ARMED WITH GOOD INTENTIONS

ARMED WITH GOOD INTENTIONS

WALLACE "WALLO267" PEEPLES
with Raquel DeJesus

GALLERY BOOKS/13A
NEW YORK LONDON TORONTO SYDNEY NEW DELHI

G 13 GALLERY BOOKS

13A/Gallery Books

An Imprint of Simon & Schuster, LLC

1230 Avenue of the Americas

New York, NY 10020

First 13A/Gallery Books hardcover edition September 2024

13A is a trademark of Charles Suitt and is used with permission.

GALLERY BOOKS and colophon are registered trademarks of Simon & Schuster, LLC

Simon & Schuster: Celebrating 100 Years of Publishing in 2024

For information about special discounts for bulk purchases, please contact Simon & Schuster Special Sales at 1-866-506-1949 or business@simonandschuster.com.

The Simon & Schuster Speakers Bureau can bring authors to your live event. For more information or to book an event, contact the Simon & Schuster Speakers Bureau at 1-866-248-3049 or visit our website at www.simonspeakers.com.

Interior design by Matt Ryan

Manufactured in the United States of America

10 9 8 7 6 5 4 3 2 1

Library of Congress Control Number: 2024028853

ISBN 978-1-6680-3625-9

ISBN 978-1-6680-3627-3 (ebook)

Dedicated to Little Steve,
Aunt Ruby, Grandmom Ora,
Uncle James,
Uncle Tommy, and Hip

CONTENTS

ARMED WITH GOOD INTENTIONS

FOREWORD

IYANLA VANZANT

THERE ARE DAYS WHEN MY soul weeps in sorrow over the number of powerful, creative, young Black men who are languishing in jail cells, on corners, or on city stoops and in cluttered backyards, totally unaware of the dynamic and divine power that lies at the center of their being, just wailing to be called forward. Then there are days when my heart breaks into a million pieces as I think about the number of young Black men who have guns and knives and bats in their hands instead of construction tools or paintbrushes or scalpels or pens. As a mother, as a grandmother, as a great-grandmother, I know how many prayers I have sent up into the highest realms to God, the Source, the Creator, the angels, and the ancestors to cover my son, my grandsons, and my great-grandson. I pray for their deliverance from the mislabeling they have received from the world that has diminished, devalued, and dehumanized them.

I pray that they are not permanently scarred in the same way that has limited and restricted the presence and power of so many Black men in the world today. Then there is, as Courtney B. Vance wrote, "the invisible ache" that seethes and festers inside of them, destroying their vision, their hope, their sense of value and worth. I pray that something, nothing short of divine, will intercede when they are burdened by the labels and misperceptions about who they are, who they are not, who they can be, and who they may never become, in a world that is both afraid and dismissive of Black men. Then there is Wallo. He is a native of Philadelphia who sat in my sorrow, who sat in my heartbreak, as I prayed. Without knowing him or that something would take hold of his spirit to guide him, to direct him, to grow him: to heal him and stretch him into the truth of his being.

While he was incarcerated, my prayers landed, without him even knowing I existed. With his mother's prayers, his grandmother's prayers, he was "infected" with a vision. I always tell my son that a vision will pull you forward. Wallo had a vision! He committed to writing it down on paper. His commitment to that vision kept his mind free. This meant that the minute his incarceration ended, he was ready to walk that vision into reality.

Wallo didn't ask permission. He simply stayed true and committed to his vision. He walked it out, taking the knocks and the bumps and the disappointment, probably seasoned with the invisible ache of fear and doubt. Yet, he never stopped walking. He spoke his truth. He turned those truths into videos that touched the ache and the sorrow, the fear and the doubt, in other young Black men who could relate to his story because they too had lived it.

And while using the media devices and tools at his disposal, he learned. And he grew. Most important, he served. Wallo is an answer to the prayer of many mothers and grandmothers. Wallo. He is a living demonstration of the powerful defiance that is required to live beyond the labels and dehumanization that so many young Black men experience. Wallo. Doing "his thing" after serving his time. Wallo. Serving other people, owning his stuff, and growing and healing in the process. Now he shares his story. He shares the steps. He shares how having a vision will pull you beyond anything you have ever done or not done; anything anyone else has said or believed about you.

Wallo is a living, breathing demonstration of the power of a focused mind. This is the same mind that exists in those young men who use guns and violence to demonstrate the pain. Wallo shares about how not to, and what happens when you refuse to allow external forces to diminish or extinguish you. Wallo shares about the value and power of allowing self-validation to grow within you, rather than seeking it externally.

Wallo, I am so proud of you. I am so happy for you. And I decree and declare the sharing of your story. The offering of this book is going to answer the prayers of many mothers and many, many grandmothers. I decree that your focused commitment will restore time and life and truth in the minds, hearts, and souls of other young Black men. You are the truth of our ancestors. Your story is the truth that will remind your brothers in the world that they are the offspring of those who chose to survive and thrive and heal and grow and serve.

Well done, my son.

Well done!

Mama Iyanla

INTRODUCTION

"The road to hell is paved with
good intentions."
—UNKNOWN

THERE WAS A TIME IN my life when quotes like the one above would mean little to nothing. They were just words written on a folded piece of paper, something you would find inside a stale fortune cookie from a run-down Chinese spot around the way. I could remember hearing phrases like this mumbled under the breath of a few slick-mouthed old heads. "Old head" is a name we call the older dudes, the ones who are usually washed-up and phased out of the game, whether by choice or by force. For the most part, many of them are disgustingly bitter, salty, broken down by their time in the streets, and angry that they never became who they wanted to be. So instead they picked up the sport of hating on the next young, up-and-coming player like it was their full-time career. Those same old heads likely predicted my downfall like some kind of ghetto prophets or more like forgotten hood heroes. Maybe I should've taken their hate as a warning that my time was surely coming. Maybe they knew something I didn't. Either way, the weight of these words had zero effect on me—until they did. And by that time, it was already too late.

FIRST DAY OUT

1

ON THE MORNING OF SATURDAY, February 18, 2017, I walked out of a state prison in Northumberland County, Pennsylvania, as a free man.

Well, not exactly.

Though I physically stood on the other side of the gates of the penitentiary, I am on parole until 2048. Let me break down for y'all what this means.

When you are convicted of a crime and the judge hands down a sentence, you receive a minimum and maximum. The *minimum* sentence is the time you're mandated to serve before you can even be considered by the parole board for early release. Your *maximum* sentence is the most amount of time you have to serve before you have satisfied your debt to society. In 2002, when I was twenty-three years old, I was given an indeterminate sentence of thirteen and a half to twenty-seven years for committing armed robbery. Unlike a determinate, where the sentence a judge gives can't be reviewed or changed by a parole board or any other agency, because my sentence had a fixed minimum of thirteen and a half, I served fifteen of those years. But when I was granted early release, I agreed to be on parole until 2048. Pennsylvania has this stipulation around parole where the amount of time you get is twice the years of the time served. So, I'm not exactly a "free man."

That reality was why I could barely feel the crisp air in my all-black Nike sweatsuit and matching black huaraches that my younger brother Troy sent me before I got out. While I was happy to wear clothes that weren't issued by the state, that day was the scariest of my life. Parole meant that any little infraction resulted in the loss of my fragile freedom. On top of that, I also knew I had to make good on the decade and a half of letters and phone calls to my grandma Nanny, mom, and family promising that this time would be different.

"How you feel?" my sister from another mister, Latifah, who drove up to get me, asked several times on the drive home.

"Good as shit!" I responded.

On the two-and-a-half-hour drive from prison back to North Philly, we stopped at a McDonald's where I inhaled an Egg McMuffin, hash browns, and a medium orange juice, savoring every bite. Our next stop was Walmart, where I was able to buy real razors to shave my face. When we got to Nanny's house, it was still light out. She was in the living room, and when I walked in, she hugged me and I felt like that little boy who used to eat scrapple and grits, messing with the antennae on the television to watch Saturday morning cartoons with my older brother, Stevie.

"I'm so happy that you're home," Nanny said. Releasing me from her embrace, Nanny stared into my eyes. Beneath her camouflaged joy was a palpable sadness. The worry on her face said it all: *I hope you get this right.*

Nanny had every right to feel this way toward me. For the past twenty-seven years, I had been in and out of juvenile detention centers, jails, police precincts, and prisons. I had dropped out of school, sold drugs, and robbed people. I had given her my word, swearing to her that the last time would be the last time, only for it to be more of the same. In the face of Nanny's doubt was my own helplessness, because I understood that nothing in that moment would help her feel different about my past behavior. Louder than any words, my actions would now have to speak for themselves.

In that homecoming week, people around the neighborhood blessed me with a couple dollars here, some clothes there. Between the money I had saved up from working various jobs in prison and the money friends and family gave, I had about $1,000. Sitting there looking at the money, I thought to myself, *I spent most of my life in jail not just because I was a risk-taker, but because I often bet against myself.*

In devoting a great deal of my life to finding the fastest route to money, I gambled with two precious assets that you don't get back when you lose that gamble: your time and your life. I'd be lying if I said I didn't win some hands, but I would also be lying if I failed to admit that my biggest wins while leading a life of crime did not compare to the losses when I got caught. In the state of Pennsylvania, 64.7 percent of formerly incarcerated people reoffend within the first three years of their release. Nearly half of that recidivism comes within just a year and a half of release.[1] One way to look at this is that the odds are literally against me, but another way to look at this is

---

1   Bucklen, Kristofer Bret, Michele Sheets, Chloe Bohm, Nicolette Bell, Jessica Campbell, Robert Flaherty, and Kate Vander Wiede. "Recidivism 2022 Report." Pennsylvania Department of Corrections, 2022. https://www.cor.pa.gov/About%20Us/Statistics/Documents/Reports/Recidivism%202022%20Report.pdf.

playing the numbers. If my chances of reoffending drop with every year I am out, the point now is to never go back.

Fortunate to still have breath in my body, I sat on my bed, painfully ashamed of the time that was gone forever—but for the first time in my life, I was equally optimistic about the fact that I had an opportunity to do something I had never done before: bet on myself.

If I could transfer the hustler's energy that I brought to robbing, stealing, and dealing to motivating people to give one hundred percent to reaching their highest potential while staying out of trouble, I thought to myself, *can't nobody fuck with me.*

BROTHER'S GONNA WORK IT OUT

2

WHEN I WAS GROWING UP in North Philly, people in the neighborhood always fucked with me. Whether they were calling me "Wally," "Little Wally," or "Little Moo Mo," they always showed me love. I was always hyper, funny, and had energy. In a neighborhood where the gears of poverty, crime, and addiction can make the sunniest day feel gray, someone who could put a smile on your face was a valued asset in our community. When everyone saw the thunderstorm on the horizon, I was always the one who could spot the peek of light breaking through.

I was born in 1979, the second child to Jacqueline "Jackie" Peeples, a nurse who worked more hours than I thought the day allowed. The eighties were rough. My father, Wallace "the People's Peeples" Peeples, was a street hustler who was admired in North Philly for his ability to make things happen by any means necessary. His face was handsomely framed by a dark goatee and neatly trimmed beard. He was a Black man in the early seventies dressed to the nines, pushing a gang of custom-kit Benzes and Rolls-Royces with diamond-flooded pinky rings to match. Tales of his generosity were as storied as what he did for himself. No story has ever been told by anyone—not his friends, family, or neighbors around the way—that didn't paint him as a man at the top of his class. I grew up knowing that this was the man I shared a name with; I would do anything to hear people talk about me with the reverence they held for him.

But two years after I was born, he disappeared. Everyone who knew my father said that his right-hand man was killed about a week prior. Though no one has ever been able to offer any concrete information or anything definitive about what happened to my father, it's not rocket science to do basic math. But still, there isn't a day that goes by that I don't wonder, at least for a quick moment, where my father is. *Is he happy? Does he have another family? Did he have to flee the country to escape a sentence?* I realize that many of my unanswered questions are mistakenly cemented in my youthful delusion. And I didn't realize until I was halfway through my fifteen-year sentence that for most of my life I had been trying to fill the void left by his absence.

My dad left us in the family home in Nicetown, Philadelphia, better known as "Ain't Nothing Nice Town"—a lower-middle-class area that had a fair amount of working-class people. Many, if not most, people living there had jobs and refused to subscribe to the streets; that wasn't something many of us were willing to admit. But for those of us whose family members were deep in the game, keeping your feet on steady ground could feel like walking on quicksand: it was just a matter of time before you fell in.

☐ ☐ ☐

AS OFTEN AS THE POOR neighborhoods are depicted as these volatile places where things happen without rhyme or reason, anyone from the hood knows that besides the occasional fight, shootout, argument, or police raid, most days are uneventful. And this is where the hood legend comes in. A hood legend is anyone whose presence and behavior inspired a certain level of respect because they did things you didn't see every day—and the stories told about them held your imagination hostage. They were a part of the community. When I was about six, there was an old head in my neighborhood who went by the name Karate Earl—and he was a hood legend.

When I say "old head," it's important to understand that I'm not writing about a man who's in his 60s, with gray hair who may qualify for social security, though that can sometimes be the case. An "old head" in this case applied to anyone older than you who served as a role model or mentor. So when I tell you Karate Earl was an old head, I can't tell you how old he really was. I just knew he was older than me. There were stories that Earl fought in Vietnam, which means that by the time I met him, in 1985, he had to be at least in his 30s, but at the same time, Earl was ageless.

Earl used to walk around the neighborhood on his tippy toes in kung fu slippers, with a scarf tied around his head, with a straight ponytail, teaching martial arts to whoever wanted to learn. He might have jeans or some slacks on, but was always in karate mode. While there were people in the neighborhood who thought Earl was crazy and laughed at him in private, whether it was a combination of fear or awe, they never disrespected him.

The day I first met Earl, he was sitting on a corner with his legs folded. Now picture this: a Black man in the middle of North Philly amongst hustlers and dealers, sitting like the statue of Buddha. On top of this, no one fucked with him. It was as if he had this force field that protected him from his surroundings. What's also important to understand is that this was the same year that Berry Gordy's *The Last Dragon* dropped. Not since Jim Kelly, the actor and martial artist who starred in blaxploitation films like *Black Belt Jones* and *Three the Hard Way*, had Black people had someone who looked like us doing martial arts. Jim Kelly's most famous role was in *Enter the Dragon*, where he starred alongside Bruce Lee. Though I knew of Jim Kelly, I didn't really connect with him as much as "Bruce" Leroy Green, played by actor Taimak in *The Last Dragon*. While Kelly was for the old heads, Bruce Leroy was closer to my age and his story resonated with me.

In the film, Bruce Leroy is a Black teenager living in Harlem who idolized Bruce Lee and aspired to become a master martial artist like him. With his training complete, Bruce Leroy's master sends him out into the world so that Leroy can achieve this coveted level of skill where his entire body would glow. You can imagine, then, that I saw Karate Earl as the man who would help me become a master.

What I remember immediately about my meeting was that he took me seriously when I asked if he could teach me. As a kid, adults, especially those who didn't always have my best interest at heart, would either dismiss my attempts to engage or try to take advantage of the fact that I was younger than them. What made my interactions with Earl special was that he didn't use my age as reason to treat me like I didn't matter; he engaged my interest as sincere and taught me what he knew. I have vivid memories of practicing what I learned from Earl, who called me "Wally," in the mirror, shirtless. To get the effect of the glow that Bruce Leroy had in the movie, I covered my entire upper body in baby oil.

Earl was a bad motherfucker—and it wasn't just because he was the first person I ever met who practiced martial arts, or because he spent time with me. In a neighborhood where it was easier to be what you saw, Earl had the courage to be who he wanted. Though I admired Earl—I sometimes wished he was my father and wanted to be like him—I was young and vulnerable to the forces of wanting to fit in with kids my age, and they weren't feeling the karate.

"Nah nigga," some of my friends from around the way would say when they saw me with Earl. "That shit is corny."

Even though people had their opinions about my hanging around Earl, my shift in focus to the streets came when my mother, Jackie, moved out of my Nanny's house in 1984, when I was five years old. That was when I lost my glow, and it would take a lifetime to get it back.

WHEN I TURNED NINE, STEVIE, who was fourteen at the time, and I were in the upstairs room listening to Public Enemy's "Louder than a Bomb" from *It Takes a Nation of Millions to Hold Us Back* on the speakers that Stevie's father, my stepfather, Hip, left us before he went to prison. Now these speakers were loud! Remember that scene in *Do the Right Thing* when Radio Raheem made those Puerto Rican dudes turn down their music because his stereo was better? Let's just say that if Stevie and I were in that movie, Radio Raheem would've been the one to turn *his* shit off.

My mom, my two brothers, and I lived at 4504 N. 17th Street in a hunter-green house, the only one on the colorful block with an indoor porch. Something I learned later in life: most people from uppity cities call indoor porches "sunrooms" or some shit like that, but not us.

My mother came home from work, and at the time, our youngest brother, Jalil, was still drinking Similac baby formula. Back then those cans were heavy enough to be used as weights. We were supposed to help her with the groceries when she came home, but the music was so loud we couldn't hear her. What we *did* hear was her screaming in pain when one of the cans of Similac fell on her foot. The scream cut through the blare of the speakers. In panic, we both ran downstairs.

"Little Stevie and Wally, help me up the stairs and get me some ice."

Once we helped her upstairs and into her room, our mother called her job telling them she wouldn't be able to make it to work the next day. That night, Stevie woke me up.

"Listen Wally, man, it's time for you to step up."

"What are you talking about?"

"Ma's foot is busted, and she can't work. So now you got to do your part and help me out. Let's go!"

For the real OGs back in the day, taking care of home was high on the list of priorities. That's unlike today, when cats like to floss for the gram or blow a bag of money trying to impress a bunch of nobodies and slide back home empty-handed. Like a dummy! Back then, you wouldn't be respected by anyone if you weren't holding down your family. That included your friends, your mistress, and your side hoes, too. For me and Stevie, that meant each other, our mom, Jalil, and Nanny.

NOW, LIKE MOST PEOPLE WHO have older siblings they admire, I saw Stevie as Superman. The two things Stevie had that I wanted the most: the ladies in the neighborhood treating him like a member of New Edition, and how to put that shit on and get fly. Stevie had a gift for making everything he wore seem as though it had been made especially for him. One of my favorite outfits of his was this navy blue Fila suit he'd wear with the matching navy blue Fila Natures with the red stripe. What stood out about that outfit wasn't that he was the only one who wore it—it was 1989, so damn-near anyone who was getting money fast was wearing it. It was the fact that he made the shit look like an Armani suit when he wore his.

I spent so many hours watching my brother get dressed, admiring every move he made. In addition to the clothes and girls, some of my greatest moments with him were listening to music in the crib because he had all the tapes. This is the dude who really put me on to everything—and now my hero wanted me to be his sidekick. By then, Stevie was already a good five years deep into snatching, stealing, boosting—and five years in the game is like dog to human years: he was a veteran by then. "Boosting" and "busting a route" is just what Philly kids called it when they were about to cause havoc and rob a local jewelry store, the mall, or even a fast-food joint.

There was a part of me that felt pressure because I didn't want to disappoint Stevie, and another part of me that was confused because this would be my first time doing this. *Do I even know how to snatch somebody's chain?* But then there was also a deeper part of me, the part that wanted the admiration I saw people who were like my father get because America loves the successful criminal.

I first learned this at FSU—Fun Step University. Keep this in mind: when I was a kid sitting on the front steps of my house, my role models weren't working folks because they just weren't around; they were at work. If they weren't at work, they were either coming from or headed to work, so they were not a consistent presence in my childhood understanding of my neighborhood. Then there were all the people who I believed were lying to me because they'd tell us "Stay in school," but everyone I knew treated the working people like stepchildren. I'd watch people come home from their long-ass shifts, tool belts slung over their shoulders, feet looking like they hurt from wearing them heavy-ass steel-toe boots, no fresh cuts, grizzly beard, smelling like a hard day, and then the adults I saw wouldn't even acknowledge them.

In contrast, when the hustler pulled up in the Benz wearing a pinky ring and anchor chains, smelling and looking like money, with the Kangol, blasting Cameo's "Candy," the same adults would fawn over the hustlers. So, in my mind, I had to become a criminal. I was going to be cool, too.

"Fuck it, man," I told Stevie. "It's game time."

LATER THAT NIGHT, WE WENT to Broad Street, where the trains and buses are—the highest concentration of people, which meant the likelihood of catching someone slipping was at its highest, and with all the people, it was easy to lose someone who might want to chase me. Standing out there, I was immediately overwhelmed. My heart was punching through my chest because I didn't know how it was going to turn out. I looked for someone who was least likely to chase after me—the person whose shock of having their jewelry taken would overwhelm their indignance. I saw this girl with her chain exposed, and my impulse kicked in.

Once I got away with the first one, the rush of doing something I knew was wrong but not being punished for it was a feeling only rivaled by my first orgasm. I was fueled enough to keep going until the fateful day of my first arrest just nine days after my eleventh birthday.

☐ ☐ ☐

AFTER TWO YEARS OF SNATCHING chains and not getting caught, I was feeling like the Mike Tyson of North Philly: unfuckwitable. That day, June 30, 1990, I was standing on the corner of Thirteenth and Allegheny, hanging out like I ain't just snatched this girl's chain. And the wild thing about it is that after getting away with shit for so long, the idea that I did something wrong occurred to me less and less. So of course when the girl's aunt, this older Black woman, grabbed me up by my collar, I was legitimately confused.

"What did I do?" I asked the woman hemming me up.

"You know what you did, you little shit!"

Just as it occurred to me to run, an officer rolled up, jumped out, and threw the cuffs on me. It was the grinding click of the handcuffs that snapped me back into reality, and I felt the embarrassment of being caught in front of the neighborhood. Now I wish I could say that being arrested at eleven in front of everyone who knew me was the source of my embarrassment, but nah. I knew this meant that Nanny was going to find out.

PHILADELPHIA
POLICE DEPARTMENT

REPORT DATE:
6/30/90

ORIGIN AND DETAILS:
A. Saturday, 6/30/90, 5:00PM, an arrest for robbery, 25th district.

B. Victim

C. P/O Tom Gaul #9492, 25th district. 2-C arrested the actor and submitted the 75-48.

INTERVIEWS AND INTERROGATIONS:
A. Victim B/F was interviewed and related the following: stated that she was coming back from the store (with her cousin) b/f. They were at Gtn. Ave. and Hilton St. when three males came up to her. One of the males asked her for her phone number, and she looked at him and kept walking. Stated that at this time the one male grabbed her shoulder, held it, and pulled her gold chain from her neck, an 18" herring bone valued at $250.00. All three males then ran west on Tioga St. from Gtn. Ave. Stated that she got in contact with her aunt, who went to Gtn. Ave. and Tioga St. and met her. She described the males to her and they went looking for them and found the male who took her chain, at 13th & Allegheny Ave. Her aunt held the male until the police arrived.

B. The aunt B/F reports that as a result of what her niece Takara said, they went to 13th and

Allegheny Ave. Where Takara identified the male who took her chain. She grabbed him and held him for the police.

C. The cousin reports that she observed the male grab her cousin's chain and run. She further identified him to her aunt at 13th and Allegheny, and to the police officer.

D. P/O Tom Gaul #9492, 25th dist. reports that at approx. 5:10pm he responded to a radio call to Gtn. and Hilton, a robbery in progress. Upon arrival the complainant identified a male later identified as Wallace Peeples 11/b/m as the one who snatched her chain. The officer arrested him and transported him to the 25th district.

NANNY

3

M **Y MOTHER'S MOTHER, LOIS PEEPLES,** is my Nanny. For thirty-one years, Nanny worked for the ERNO Products Company as the head of bottling inventory. The epitome of a hard worker, Nanny only missed forty-one days during those three decades.

Nanny and I have a bond unlike any other I've known. She's *thurl* (Philly slang for "thorough")—thurl and tough yet soft as a bed of clouds. She is wise and hip to the game, yet I can talk to her for hours, and she'll still seem intensely interested in everything I have to say, as if it's her first time hearing many things. She stands about five three and has always been beautiful, her skin smooth like butter and mahogany. You could place any bottle style within a mile of her eyes, and she would call out the model number, shape, and size. "That's a Cylinder, shorty neck, thirty-millimeter cap," she'd snap. Nanny is the backbone of the family. She believed in me when no one else did.

Growing up in a time when a girl who enjoyed sports was considered a "tomboy," her earliest aspiration was to become a coach for a women's basketball team or physical education teacher. I share these details to give you the sense that Nanny wasn't one of the traditional grandmothers who wore a muumuu and slippers. She always wore jeans and sneakers.

Nanny is a loving person. Nanny is kind. Nanny is gentle. Nanny is assertive. But one of the things I used to love was when I was about five or six, she made me grits with either bacon or scrapple on the side. That was the greatest shit ever. I used to be happy sitting at the table. She had these hard black skillets she prepared the meals in.

Some of my earliest, most special memories before the shame and anger set in go back to spending summer days with my grandmother. Nanny's house was like a playground to me. There was nothing I couldn't dream up and bring to life when I stayed there. It was a decent-sized row home off Thirteenth Street. The first floor was where Nanny sat in her La-Z-Boy and watched her game shows.

One time as a kid I was upstairs, pretending to be some kind of ghetto superhero, jumping from bed to bed, crashing into the furniture and walls in nothing more than my tighty-whities and a towel wrapped around my neck like a cape. I could hear Nanny downstairs in the kitchen cooking up something for us to eat. I wondered what she was making, but I didn't want to go down and ask because she might have something for me to do. Nanny didn't play games when it came to doing what she told you needed to be done. If me and my siblings were acting up and not doing as we were told, she wouldn't hesitate to pull out her three-inch-thick cowboy belt and whoop our ass with it like Indiana Jones. Damn, I can still remember the welts like it was yesterday. After one round of licks, you would swear you got pistol-whipped.

"Wallace, what the hell is all that noise up there? Get your butt down here right now!" Nanny called out. I flew down the stairs so fast, not even thinking about the fact that I didn't have a stitch of clothes on to shield me if I was going to get lit up. My eyes shot wide open when I saw that metal buckle.

"Yes, Nanny. I was just playing around," I stammered, out of breath from acting a fool upstairs. Nanny took one look at me and fell out laughing.

"Boy, if you don't go ahead and shower, put some dang clothes on, and get ready to eat . . ." She could barely finish what she was saying before she started cracking up again. "I'm making your favorite, apple pound cake," she said between her laughter. That was the moment I knew I wanted to give the world to her if I could.

Nanny always knew just the right thing to say. If I had questions about life, girls, or anything, Nanny would have an answer for me. She'd answer practically anything, straight no chaser, just how she liked her whisky. There was always something special that made me feel fuzzy when the smell of warm whisky wrapped around her glowing brown skin.

In the summers, between the ages of three and ten, we would ride down to her hometown of Seaford, Virginia, to visit Great-Grandma Lee, short for Liola, who was Nanny's mother, in Nanny's tan Monte Carlo station wagon. On those long rides down to the countryside, I would come up with what seemed like a million questions just to hear the tone of her voice.

"Nanny, do you think I'm smart?" I once asked with genuine curiosity.

"Of course I do, baby. You're smart, and you're sharp, just like your granny. But you just don't like to act right," she responded while gently shaking her head. "Wally-O, you have to start acting right and behave yourself in school and everywhere else, or it's going to catch up to you someday soon." Her voice would crackle slightly and drift off, almost like she could see the road I was heading down better than the winding I-95 ahead of her.

My mother was young—only twenty-two—when she had me, so she was more like my sister growing up. So back then, I regarded Nanny as my mother. For a long time, I didn't understand the role that age plays in parenting, and how our parents are still trying to figure out who they are when they have us. My mother, although she loved me the best way she knew how, seemed apathetic and never quite as warm or nurturing as my grandmother and great-grandmother. Maybe it had something to do with my mom being raised outside the reach of the friendly peach-country skies and under the cold, Gotham City–like gray Philadelphia clouds; maybe it was just that she was still growing up herself.

Those trips to Virginia showed me how different life could be. It would always amaze me on those drives down how different the trees appeared in all their shapes, colors, and sizes. Bright yellow, orange, and green leaves would dance and wave at us as we passed by, and somehow the sun would reflect off them and bounce off the hood of the car and into my lap during the long stretch of southern miles. I would take in every detail. The air was crisp and fresh like the apples in Nanny's pound cake, and the clouds seemed to stay far behind us in Philadelphia. Leaving city life behind, even if it was just for a weekend, gave me clarity and peace of mind. I was free to see things as they were, the beauty in nature surrounding us and the empty canvas on which to imagine just about anything of the ocean-blue sky. And best of all, the loving looks I would catch in the rearview mirror from Nanny's chocolate-brown eyes.

"Aye, Wally-O." Those were the first words I would hear, like a song being sung by an angel, once we arrived. Great-Grandma Lee was always there to greet me with open arms and the most tender, gleaming smile that could light up the whole town.

You'd be surprised by how quickly I would adjust to country life.

"Slow down, boy," Great-Grandma Lee would say as I would rush her back into the house, where we would pull together all the items we needed to make our famous sun tea.

"Granny, we have to hurry before the sun goes down, and we won't be able to make our tea," I would blurt out excitedly.

"Don't worry; you know I always have a pitcher ready for you when you get here, child," Granny said, her high cheekbones becoming more visible with her stunning smile. But it wasn't about the tea or even about being thirsty after a long ride from the city. It was the process of making something together and seeing something I created come to life to share with everybody.

"Mason jars, check. Tea bags, check. Water, check. And last but not least, sugar, check," I would rattle off the list of ingredients to be brought outside to the shed kitchen behind the house, being mindful not to forget any items while running back and forth. Great-Grandma Lee's house was built by a white family whose children she raised. My great-grandmother was someone else's *nanny*, caring for children who looked nothing like us while her children waited for her past sundown, but that's what was required to keep a roof above all our family's heads.

Great-Grandma Lee had beautiful long silver hair that would glisten in the sun like tinsel on a Christmas tree. At night as we sat on the porch drinking a cold glass of sun tea, Nanny would comb Granny Lee's hair and grease her scalp. When she was done massaging and adding moisture to her shining hair, Nanny would braid her hair in two long braids parted down the middle. Her braids nearly reached the ground.

I asked, "Granny, how'd you get your hair so long like that?"

"Well, it shows how much wisdom I got. And let them tell it, our people are Geechie and got some kind of Indian blood running through us."

Cats and kittens swarmed the patio when the sun reached its lowest point. Unlike the city, where streetlamps would light up and give you some visibility in the shadows, here at Granny Lee's, you couldn't see more than two feet away when the sun went down. I would be lying if I said I wasn't scared to death sitting in the dark with my little gang of purring cats. The quiet and the stillness were unfamiliar. My thoughts would race—millions of them swirled through my head with nowhere to go. Later in life, I discovered the swirling storms of thoughts I tried to calm stemmed from attention deficit disorder, which went misdiagnosed and untreated.

The ride back to Philly was always bittersweet. It felt as if we spent just enough time for me to miss running the streets but never enough time to forget the problems that went along with it. I was so young and confused by the pushing and pulling of my own mental state. I knew I wanted to do great things to make my family proud, and I definitely wanted to be *the man* as far back as I could remember. I wanted to be Robin Hood of the hood. Whoever needed something, I wanted to be the one with pockets loaded enough to get it for them. But I didn't grasp the reality that I was only a kid. So when things got tight around the house, or friends didn't have money to eat, that shit would tear a hole through my chest.

"Baby," my Nanny used to tell me often, "when you stop moving, you stop moving." At that point in my life, Nanny knew I was a knucklehead and did her best to rear me in the direction that would benefit me long term.

But June 30, 1990, was different. When we arrived at the precinct, Nanny was the first person they called. "Oh my God, what the hell you done do?"

She sent my uncle Tommy to come get me. Now that I'm older, I understand the impact of somebody young getting arrested. If I now heard that my eleven-year-old nephew got arrested, I would be devastated, but I had no frame of reference for this back then.

Now, my uncle Tommy wasn't on the streets. I used to be in his room in Nanny's house, man, just listening to eight tracks and comedy albums, everything from Redd Foxx to Richard Pryor. He'd be rolling his weed, which he always called "reefer," on the records. He was the neighborhood handyman, always fixing things here and there, but he managed to stay out of the way.

When we got back to Nanny's house, of course she was pissed, but even then, I could see more fear and disappointment, even helplessness, in her face. At that point she had not yet retired, and she was doing what she could to hold on to the life she had. After her husband, my grandfather, Charles Vincent Peeples, who served in the military, caught himself raising his hand to Nanny, she got his ass up and kicked him out of there.

But as resilient as my beautiful Nanny was, and as hard as she beat me that day for snatching that girl's necklace, and as much as she reminded me that I knew right from wrong, my head was already harder than my ass at that point. I would get arrested two more times within a month for the same shit. Nanny would shake her head.

"I don't know when, or what, but one day you're going to learn, and I hope you do before it's too late."

I spent many of my childhood years in and out of juvenile detention. It was almost like I was a boxer training for my big bid. Except I couldn't fight to save my life! I spent two years, from 1990 to 1992, at St. Michael's School for Boys in Tunkhannock, Pennsylvania. It was a program meant to instill discipline and direction in misguided youth in hopes of successful reentry into society—all of which was pure bullshit. The most they ever did for kids like me was shove board games in our faces and leave us alone long enough for us to plot our next criminal stint. There wasn't a single adult, counselor, or therapist inclined to question why I was doing what I was doing or what it was about my environment that continuously influenced me to make the decisions leading me down the path to ruin. For many of them, this was just a paycheck with a hefty pension waiting for them not too far down the road.

Back then, I didn't even know what anxiety was, but I knew I was angry—or more like pissed-the-fuck-off. Anger always boiled just below the surface, and I desperately wanted to go into full-on rage and bark at them. *Just say it from your chest! Say it to my face! What? Oh, you think I'm dumb? You don't think I'm worth my fucking freedom!* All these clashing sound bites bounced off the walls of my mind as counselors wrote their little notes and opinions of me. Fortunately for them, I couldn't fully express myself how I wanted to without fear of further punishment, so I would mentally drift off, awkwardly staring into space for the remainder of our sessions.

Quarterly Review
of Service Plan

PERIOD COVERED:
June 1991 to August 1991

NAME:
Wallace Peeples

AGE:
12

PRESENTING PROBLEMS/REASON FOR REFERRAL:
Wallace Peeples was referred to St. Michael's
Residential Program by Philadelphia County Juvenile
Probation. Wallace was adjudicated delinquent
on charges of robbery, simple assault, reckless
endangerment, and receiving stolen property. It is
noted that Wallace Peeples is being handled by the
Habitual Offenders Unit of the Philadelphia County
Juvenile Probation Department. Wallace was admitted
to St. Michael's on 9-19-1990.

1. Wallace has shown some difficulty in accepting
   responsibility for his actions. At times, he
   relies on denial or projection to minimize
   accountability.

2. Wallace has demonstrated impulsive behaviors
   with little thought to the consequences of
   those behaviors for himself and others.

3. Wallace seems to be experiencing low self-
   esteem as manifested in the impaired ability to
   form appropriate relationships with others, a
   tendency to be a follower, a lack of goals, and
   inconsistent motivation for self-improvement.

4. Wallace appears to resist having limits or structure imposed upon him. He has little insight into the need for order, structure, and accountability.

5. Wallace is in need of a trusting relationship with adult role models to provide him with emotional support on a consistent basis that will allow him the opportunity to verbalize his feelings.

Quarterly Review
of Service Plan

PERIOD COVERED:
7-29-92 to 10-29-92

AREAS OF INTERVENTION:
Wallace has demonstrated impulsive behaviors
with little thought to the consequences of these
behaviors for himself or others.

METHODOLOGY:
A combination of counseling and behavioral
management approaches will be utilized to improve
self-control and to provide positive reinforcement
for thoughtful, planned behaviors.

GOAL AND TARGET DATE:
Wallace will develop a better ability to consider
alternatives and to recognize and consider the
consequences of his behavior.

TARGET DATE:
Ongoing

PERSON(S) RESPONSIBLE:
Wallace

Social Worker

Treatment Team

CURRENT STATUS:

Impulse control on Wallace's part continues to be a major concern. This is no more evident than by Wallace's actions previously noted on the weekend of 8/7 thru 8/9. Wallace's rearrest and reinvolvement in delinquent activity goes to the point that he clearly remains at risk for poorly planned and poorly thought-out kinds of activities.

HIGHS AND LO

4

ONE WEEKEND THAT I WAS home from Vision Quest in '94, a juvenile detention center for troubled youth that used Native American philosophy and ceremonies to teach us character, I was in downtown Philly with my homeboy Little Larry (RIP). While I waited outside, he walked into this jewelry store with dummy money. All the money was real, but he wrapped the biggest bill we had—a $50 or a $20—around $200 to $300 worth of singles wrapped in a rubber band. When Larry flashed the money to make it look like he had enough, he pointed at the chain he wanted. Once the jeweler placed the chain on Larry's neck, I motioned the door to get buzzed in. As soon as the door was buzzed, Larry ran out. That day in the store, we were pulling the stunt when I peeped a dude looking through the window. I didn't recognize him. We busted a move out of the jewelry store, and he ran behind us. So now I was alert and slowed down. The bul had this heavy New York accent. "Boul," "bol," or "bul" is Philly slang for a man, especially a young one. It's a term that casts a wide net and is how many people in Philly refer to one another, like how New Yorkers use "son" or surfers refer to each other as "dude."

"No, no, no. It's cool, son. Word up. It's cool."

He pulled some money out of his pocket and introduced himself.

"Yo son, I'm B-Bill from Brooklyn. Lo Life."

The "B" in his name stood for "Boostin,' " and he was a member of Lo Life, a group started by some thorough dudes in Brooklyn who bonded over a shared aspiration of boostin' and rocking the newest Ralph Lauren pieces. Part of the appeal was that they weren't buying their rare pieces of Polo; they were stealing them. Like the hustlers who grew up in the projects but managed to pull up in a Mercedes-Benz, part of the flex of being a Lo Life was rocking something you weren't supposed to have. The swagger was bold and defiant. And the hustle with boosting was twofold: when you stole clothes, you brought your gains back to the hood and flipped it to someone at a discount. What did it matter? It was all profit to us.

After B-Bill introduced himself, Larry told me he was taking the chain to a pawn shop and that we'd bust down the profits later. B-Bill was head to toe in Lo. He was the first motherfucker I saw with the high-top beef and broccoli field Timbs, the first dude I saw with dreads. Before B-Bill, the only dudes I knew who had dreads were the Rastas. While we were walking down Market Street, we walked into City Blue, a streetwear store that sold all the fly shit—including Polo.

"Son, I'm telling you son, just walk with me. Word up. I ain't with no bullshit, word to my mother."

Now, he had on this long flannel Polo trench. B-Bill took three Pelle jackets, wrapped them up while they were still on the hanger, and stuffed them up his back between the jacket and the shirt he was wearing.

"Jump on my back, son."

Even though I ain't peep why he asked me to jump on his back, I did what he told me.

"Yo, man, stop fucking playing man. You always playing. I'm telling Mommy!"

A sales associate rushed over. "Get out of the store, playing!"

When we went out of the store, he swung me around. I hit the alarm box with my leg. The alarm went off, but the sales associate cared more about us getting out of the store than figuring out what set the alarm off.

Right in front of the store was the subway. So he walked toward the entrance. He was still in character.

"Yo man, stop fucking playing."

We went down the stairs, and he folded up the jackets and handed me one.

"What's your name, son?"

"Lil Wally."

"Nah, son," B-Bill said. "Your name is Wal-Lo."

HER NAME WAS VERONICA SMITH. We were both fourteen. She lived in uptown Philly. She was a beautiful light-skinned girl. That was the first girl to make me cry—my introduction to love. At this point I'm out here boosting, stealing clothes. This was in 1993, between one of my stints at Vision Quest. When I wasn't out on probation, I was back in juvie.

I was with one of the homies, and she was with her girls. And I walked over to her. I was one of those dudes that was always funny, so I said some shit like:

"Damn Slimmy, what's up?"

She laughed and looked me up and down.

"Boy, I don't even know you!"

I spent time around older dudes like Stevie who knew how to get with women, knew how to dress, knew how to smell good, and had a mouthpiece. They knew exactly what to say, when and how.

But I really wasn't a player. I was an imaginary one. A player by association. I was listening to 2 Live Crew, Ice-T, and Special Ed because my stepfather, Hip, put me down with all the classics. I was watching movies like *The Mack* and reading Iceberg Slim's *Pimp* and Donald Goines. When I went in my room, I'd look in the mirror and rap these songs to myself, attempting to embody the persona these rappers projected in their lyrics. People that know me always say I'm the greatest at lip synching. But singing other people's words is easy; coming up with your own is hard. When it came to Veronica, I was terrycloth soft. I wasn't cold enough. But the biggest truth was I wanted to be loved more than I wanted to be a player. And most of the time I would get shot down because I wasn't going for just any chick—I was going for the tens. And I would shoot at a grown-ass woman because you missed a hundred percent of the shots you don't take.

In the early nineties, you never left the crib without a pen. You never knew who you were going to see, and a pen guaranteed that chance encounters lasted longer than a few moments. And this is back when I used to wear the pen-pocket Polo, Guess, or Girbaud jeans and New Balances. I don't remember what I said to get Veronica to laugh, but I do know I made her laugh hard enough to write my number down using my pen.

Next thing you know, we were on the phone all the time. And the thing is, Ronnie (my nickname for her) would talk on the phone until we fell asleep. She was taking the bus down to the neighborhood just to kick it with me. We were sitting on the steps, holding hands in the park, all that soft shit. One day we got into an argument, and I remember being more Iceberg Slim than myself.

"You hurt my feelings. I'm leaving," she said.

And she left. Emotionally I was sick, but on the surface I was acting cool. At first, I went in the house and waited the twenty minutes it would take for her to get back home to call her. I kept calling to see if she got in the house, and nobody else was there. The phone kept ringing. Right at that point, the lyrics to New Edition's "Mr. Telephone Man" started playing in my head: *"Must be a bad connection, I give her my love and affection."* After what felt like an hour, Ronnie finally answered.

"What you want?"

"Please, can you please come back?"

"No. You hurt my feelings."

In the entirety of my life at that point, I hadn't experienced anyone who was so in touch with their feelings and felt that they mattered enough to advocate for themself. Most of us were so busy regarding our feelings as liabilities—we didn't know, or bother to learn, how to understand them. And here was Ronnie, telling me I hurt something I didn't even think I had the capacity to. I started crying on the phone.

"I messed up. *Please don't leave me!*"

After five minutes of me breaking down like Tre in *Boyz n the Hood,* she got back on the bus. We hugged and cuddled on the couch in my basement. That's where I lost my virginity. But before I did, Ronnie was the girl who schooled me to a prerequisite:

"You got to lick it before you stick it."

That night, I enrolled. Me and her were going tough, but by 1994, I was locked back up at Vision Quest for boosting something. But the entire time I was up there, I was still hanging tough with her, calling her. I told her I'd be home soon, and they ended up hitting me with twelve months. *Small thing to a giant,* I thought to myself. Once or twice a week I wrote her letters. For that whole year in Vision Quest, I never got a letter back. The whole time, I thought that somebody at her house was hating. When I got out in the summer of 1995, the first person I had my homie drive me to see was Ronnie.

When we got back to North Philly, I knocked on her door, and she opened it.

"Damn girl. I mean, what's up?"

She comes outside where it's hot, but her warmth is gone.

"Hey, what's up?"

"Damn girl, I wrote you all them letters. Did you get them?"

"Yeah, I got them."

Right then, I felt like Martin in that scene in *Blue Streak* where he goes to see his girl after doing that prison bid for the stolen diamond and she curves him. *Don't do me like this!* But I maintained my composure. Or tried to.

"What you been up to, man?"

"Come on," she told me. "Let's walk down the street."

So we walked down the street. The entire time, I was complimenting her, telling her how good she looked. She did her best impression at a smile. In hindsight, what was about to happen was clear, but I was blinded by what I didn't want to see. Once we got to the corner of the block, she dropped a bomb on me.

"I got a man."

"What?"

In that moment my heart dropped. I wanted to cry right there. But I was too player then to realize that the only person I played was myself.

WELCOME TO THE JUNGLE

6

"**L**OOK AT THIS SKINNY, BROKE** motherfucker," I heard from behind as I walked up the block, bored and looking for something to get myself into. It was the summer of 1996. I looked over my shoulder to see the two neighborhood derelicts, Lil Shooter and Baby D, charging toward me. Lil Shooter quickly pulled his hands out of his pockets, grasped his right hand with his left, and then pointed his fingers as if they were a gun, aiming them directly at my face. He squinted his devilish hazel eyes and pulled his trigger finger back twice. "Welcome back to the block, nigga."

Hugs and kisses weren't come by easily. Shit, daps, and pounds weren't the first greetings of choice either. You'd sooner be met with a round of hooks and jabs by amateur shadowboxers than you would a fucking high five. We were hardened, big *dawgs*, tough to pet.

Lil Shooter and Baby D, who were both a few years older than me, were always attached at the hip. It was rare that you ever saw one without the other. They were worse and worst, and they took turns battling it out for who could outdo the other. Lil Shooter had the frame of a martial arts ninja. Even as a young teen, his body was intimidating. He had broad shoulders, a slim waist that formed an upside-down triangle, and solid, muscular legs. If you could imagine Bruce Lee and Flo Jo having a baby, it would be him. I bet if he wanted to, he could kick a hole through a brick wall, but he used those horse hams to run down on niggas and drop them before they could even think about busting a move. In the hood, most guys focused on doing push-ups, sit-ups, and pull-ups on monkey bars. Maybe some would pump iron here and there, but from the waist down, they were usually standing on two twigs for legs, skinny as fuck, leaving them wide open to getting slammed through the concrete by a Shooter no matter how quick they were on their feet.

That was the only area Lil Shooter and Baby D were opposite. Baby D was a chubby little fucker. He went out of his way to stay round, chubby-bodied, and sluggishly heavy, so he had an excuse to pull out his gun and shoot from down the block. It seemed like they took more pleasure in hurting anyone they could get their hands on than actually getting to the money. Most people would suggest staying as far away from them as possible. But the smart thing for me to do then was to keep those two wolves as close to me as possible and stay in their good graces. In the line of business I was in, robbing, boosting, and stealing anything I could get my hands on, it was best to have a team of vicious knuckleheads on the same side of the fence, or they would have surely made food out of me too.

"Yo! What up, playas? How you be?"

"Ain't nothing. We just came back from the trenches kicking it with some hoes," Baby D said.

"Man, shut yo fat ass up, nigga. Them hoes weren't thinking bout yo ugly ass," Lil Shooter said, laughing. "Yeah, they were fucking with me until your grimy ass walked up! They just ain't want their pussy and their purse snatched by your psycho ass." We all laughed. Without verbalizing any plans, the three of us started walking up the boulevard. It was almost as if it was an unspoken rule that finding something to do when there was nothing to do meant someone was bound to get robbed and preferably soon.

I knew I had to take the lead on things. I had to make it quick and smooth, or things could take a sharp turn for the worse. Finding an easy target, someone I could grab something of value from that wouldn't put up much of a fight, was the most ideal. As we continued walking up the crack-impacted avenue, Lil Shooter spotted a couple of the girls they were kicking it with earlier.

"There them hoes go."

Baby D and I shot each other looks of uncertainty.

"Nah, not them." But Shooter had that crazed look. And we followed suit.

I was the youngest, the fastest, and the only one that made a rule to *never harm anyone* if I didn't have to. So I darted solo in the girls' direction and ran just a few feet past them so I could snatch their handbags and necklaces from behind when they least expected it. But it didn't quite work out that way. One of the girls was Sheila, an older girl I always had my eye on. I swore I would make her mine as soon as I got a little older and got my paper up. But as soon as I sprinted across the street to get at them, startled Sheila said, "Little Wally, where you going?"

"Little?" I paused and looked at her as if she had just spit in my face. But I had no time to waste: Lil Shooter was a few paces away, and I'd rather it be just a purse and a chain than Shooter fuck up her pretty face.

"Little?" I questioned again, with a sudden twitch in my right eye. "Gimme this *little* chain then, bitch," I growled as I swiftly snatched her chain from her neck, her purse, and the shopping bags from her girlfriend, too. I took off, hauling ass back toward the guys so they could switch direction and leave the girls alone in their confusion. Lil Shooter was laughing and screaming so loud in amusement you would have thought he was trying to get us all caught by the po-po. Baby D didn't say much; he just looked at me once we stopped, like, *Damn! You know you just fucked up?*

We posted up on the side of a run-down liquor store where a used plastic bag was hanging off the door handle. I grabbed it, filled it with the purses and chains, and shoved it into Lil Shooter's ribs. "Here," I mumbled, out of breath. He looked at me with disgust.

"Fuck you giving me this for?" he asked. "Aww nigga, you pussy! Yo young ass caught up about them hoes already? I thought you were built different. You act just like this tender-dick nigga over here." He looked in Baby D's direction, and I could see that animosity brewed between them.

"Watch out, man," Baby D said, bumping into Shooter and walking off.

I said, "Naw, it's cool. I hit those come ups every day, all day; besides, yo dusty ass needs to go buy you some fresh New Balance or some shit anyway. With yo stank'n ass." I laughed and chucked up the deuces, walking off too in the other direction.

I could feel him staring at me through the back of my head, but I kept walking almost aimlessly, asking myself, *What the fuck did you just do, nut-ass nigga?* I knew robbing the girls was going to end up no good! They were the *it girls* and had more thurl brothers than a little bit. Most of them were Muslim, but that never mattered, especially when it came to handling their family business. The majority of them converted to Islam while either locked up in the penitentiary or when their dad or uncles had come back from doing a bid and brought the discipline back home. These guys would quickly go from *ahki*, the Arabic word for "brother," to your most feared enemy. Trust me, you didn't want to fuck with them. I had my share of Muslim cousins, too, so I always felt like I could get myself out of a jam if I needed to. But this wasn't the kind of war I wanted to start anytime soon. As young as I was, I still understood neighborhood wars should be prevented as much as possible.

That night, I went back to my mom Jackie's house. I couldn't deal with the thought of *ahkis* and them paying me a visit while back at Nanny's house, which is where I stayed when I wasn't at my mother's house. Going to my mother's house instead just seemed like the obvious and best choice. Besides, Jackie probably wouldn't be home even if things did take flight. I was used to spending nights alone and free to roam whenever I chose to. At this point, I knew it'd be easier not to have to answer any questions about why I'd keep peeping out the window. Quietly, I hoped my stepfather, Hip, would come by our house. There was a kind of communication we had that didn't need words. He was from the streets and easily read me like a book. He wouldn't pry or try to squeeze the juice out of me; he would just randomly start dropping gems on how to maneuver. He never approved of the stick-up kid business. He felt it was unnecessary, and it just wasn't his thing. He was part of a wrecking crew, the Center City Hustlers, and they were nothing to fuck with either. As he saw it, "A robbery ain't nothing but a murder waiting to happen."

As soon as I reached my block, the neighborhood junkies would start that begging shit. "Aye, champ, you got a lil something-something for me?" I was paranoid of everyone at this point. Back then, people used to send dope fiends over to distract you and have you focused on their shaking hands counting out your dough, and then *bam*, you're getting popped on the sly when you're fixated on a dollar and not paying attention to who and what was surrounding you.

"Man, get the fuck on somewhere," I said through gritted teeth. I was cautious not to make any major disturbances in what was considered a regular chain of events but sturdy enough for the dust head to know to at least come back later at best.

I wasn't right mentally. I recall feeling particularly uneasy about this last route. It was foreign territory to me to rob someone that I not only knew but liked, too. My stomach was still twisting in knots, and every noise or shadow I passed felt like a vital threat. Once I made it to the house, I was surprised to be greeted at the door by my mother. She opened the door and looked me up and down with elevator eyes and a harsh but knowing stance.

"Boy, what the fuck is wrong with you?"

"What's wrong with you?" I shot back with an attitude. She laughed, tossed her red-and-black leather jacket on, and headed out the door. Before closing it, she turned around and said, "Don't let anybody in my goddamned house, you hear me?" And for a very brief moment, I just wanted her to stay with me.

THREE WEEKS LATER I WAS at a house party. Back then, house parties with rooms filled with thick smoke from joints sprinkled with a dash of coke were the closest thing you would get to flying high in those times. Whether you were smoking the shit yourself or just there in the general vicinity, you were bound to become a kite for the night. Although I didn't trust it enough to partake in it as a group activity, the secondhand high was a good time, I can't lie. I liked the feeling of everything slowing down a bit in my mind. My hyperactive brain was always on a thousand. It was the welcomed shift in speed that I enjoyed the most. I was elevated like a UFO off that stank shake-and-bake smoke.

"So you just gonna stand there looking goofy, or you going to hit the J?" I heard a womanly voice say. I looked up to see who it was and who they were talking to, and it was fine-ass Michelle standing there with her girlfriends, passing me a joint.

"Naw, I'm good. I'm already high as the sky," I said, forcing my eyes to look low as if I really were. They all laughed in unison. *Shit, maybe I am already gone. I might as well hit it so these hoes don't think I'm bitch made.* "Yeah, fuck it, let me hit that."

"Hit what?" Michelle snapped back. "You wouldn't know what to do with this if I put it right under your nose, lil boy." At that moment, I realized we weren't talking about the weed anymore, and she was on the same type of time I was.

"Let me hit it and find out," I replied fast.

The living room, kitchen, and hallway were jam-packed with people from around the way. Some unfamiliar faces were there as well. You gotta understand I was at least seven to ten years younger than the majority of the guests in attendance. Honestly, I could only come through because I was known for being Steven's wild little brother but also for putting in work and keeping my mouth shut when the cops came through. Typically, the drug dealers of the time got the most praise, and folks in my line of work were looked down on because we were likely to steal from them as well. But I was different because I shared the wealth.

"Wally," I heard Michelle yell from the back room. My heart started racing. As I made my way through the crowd of dealers, killers, and pimps, I quickly smoothed down my T-shirt with my hands and licked the ash from around my lips. As I got closer, I could see the glistening chocolate calves of another woman's legs lying across the bed right behind Michelle's thighs. My mouth watered, like a dog drooling over a plate of left-out food. "Wally, you've met my girlfriend before, right?"

Before I could say no, she said, "You know, sexy-ass Sheila!" Sheila sat up, connecting direct eye contact with me.

"Hey Wally, thank you, boo," Sheila said, leaving me thoroughly confused.

Michelle tilted her head with her silky pressed hair. "Oh, so y'all have met; cool, this should be fun!"

I was too stunned to speak.

Sheila turned to Michelle. "Yeah, Wally sent my things back in a janky-ass plastic bag with Baby D the day I told you some dirtballs robbed us on the boule. I knew his ass wasn't that stupid!" While high-fiving Michelle, she laughed.

"Speak of the fucking devil," a voice said from behind me in the doorway. It was Lil Shooter and Baby D making their way toward me.

Sheila looked up and slowly shook her head, putting her finger to her lips and whispering, "Shhhh, don't say nothing!" The timing couldn't have been any less confusing.

"What up, soft-ass nigga," Lil Shooter said while pushing his fingers into the side of my head, pulling the imaginary trigger two times as he always did.

"What up, fam," I replied.

"Ain't nothing. We about to blow this joint and go get into something. You rolling?"

I nodded without hesitating, and I turned to walk out the doorway.

"Oh, shit. Baby D, ain't that yo bitch right there? Big-head-ass Sheila?" Shooter said. The five of our heads were all on swivel. We each caught a glimpse of the other, trying to make sense of everything transpiring.

Baby D smirked and sprinkled in a light laugh, saying, "Nah, man, she's cool. We ain't like that."

Lil Shooter cracked up laughing. "That's what I thought, you fat-ass nigga." And we all laughed and kept it moving, letting the tension out of the air with each step away from the room.

The streets were wet from the rain we'd missed while inside at the party. Damn, I wished I was still at that party! It was dead, and not much movement going on. Either everyone was at a house party getting some ass like I was supposed to be or laid up somewhere hiding from the sticky Philly weather. Either way, there wasn't really shit out there for us to do. So I called it.

"Aye yo, I'm outta here. I'll see ya tomorrow."

Baby D nodded in agreement and gave me a pound while Lil Shooter again pointed his fingers toward my head.

"Pop-Pop," he said. Then he smiled and laughed, "Aight, bet."

I ran toward Jackie's house, and the gruesome twosome took off in the opposite direction. Getting in and out of the streets as quickly as a bank robber was our instinctual thought process. I got less than a few feet away when I heard two gunshots, *POP-POP*. I turned around, trying to sharpen my focus, to see Baby D still running. I zeroed in on Lil Shooter—he was face down on the ground with two holes in the back of him. And I ran.

That was the moment I realized three things can turn even your best friend into your worst enemy: money, pussy, and power. I guess Sheila was Baby D's "bitch" and Shooter had to learn this vicious lesson through the art of discovery.

COMMONWEALTH OF PENNSYLVANIA
PHILADELPHIA COUNTY

COMMONWEALTH OF PENNSYLVANIA VS. WALLACE PEEPLES

The acts committed by the accused were:

At 3032 N. Broad Street, while acting in concert
with another defendant, at point of firearm, did
forcibly take property from the complainant,
Kentucky Fried Chicken

To wit: U.S.C.

Defendant is not licensed to carry a firearm

BEFORE I COULD EVEN TURN the corner into the parking lot of the chicken spot just around the block from Nanny's house, the right side of my face started twitching as usual. It was something that happened to me every time I was en route—a not-so-subtle reminder to pick up the pace and get on top of what needed to be done. I hit a light jog around the back of the restaurant, trying not to look suspicious, with my gun firmly gripped in my sweaty palm, tucked halfway in the pocket of my hoodie.

Something Hip tried to instill in me from the moment he knew I was doing my thing was that once guns come into play, there's no turning back, and everything will change. It not only changes you, but it also changes the field you're playing on.

For the most part, I agreed with him. I didn't have it in me to shoot anyone, anyway. I was far from a tough guy, and I damn sure wasn't built like that—to shoot someone or take somebody's life? Never that! Hip made sure I understood that you could always replace simple things like money, clothes, and other material shit, but life is forever gone once you take it. And up until that point, my routes were running smoothly without a gun. But then I took a wild ride with my OG, Big-Poppi, and he put me on to an entirely new way of running up the money.

Now Big-Poppi was way ahead in the robbery game. At this time, I was still figuring out quicker ways to get paid besides boosting. Hitting the shops was alright. I was doing my thing, but it took too much time to hit the racks, break up the bags, and sell whatever I could get my hands on. It all was taking too long. The OG said he wouldn't dare risk it all just to profit off scraps. And right then and there is when he pulled out the gat. He told me how much easier things could be when you carry a *piece*. He told me he could show me better than tell me, and he pulled the car over right on Twenty-Second and Indiana, right between the bank and the Video Shack.

OG didn't do too much talking. I don't even think he gave me any instructions. He just handed me the gun, and we both popped out of the car and rolled up on the money manager making his morning deposit.

"You know what this is; get to it. Empty the fucking bag and make it quick!" Big-Poppi yelled. I was stunned that there were no questions and no fights. For the first time in my young criminal life, I witnessed an armed robbery that went smoother than a bean pie getting cut by a warm knife.

That was the easiest fifteen stacks I ever made. I couldn't believe it. I almost felt stupid for wasting so much time, toeing the line trying to maintain some type of morals, and robbing without pistols to keep things clean. Meanwhile, this motherfucker just made what I'd make in a week in under five minutes without even busting a sweat. As I sat in the car, my heart still racing, I was winded and out of breath; by the time we hit the next block, my mind was already made up: *Fuck that! I got to get me a piece!*

Back at the house, I paced in circles as my mind was still blown away by what I had just accomplished. I was restless and eager to try that same shit by myself. Before this day, I had never had a gun of my own, but now I was on a mission to get one first thing in the morning.

Once I got a gun, it didn't take more than twenty-four hours before I hit the streets at least twice a week in search of a new play. In the back of my mind, I could hear Hip's words over and over: "Do your thing but leave them guns alone. One wrong move and everyone's life is gone." Those words haunted me almost every day. But the ghosts of robberies gone wrong weren't quick enough to catch up with the thrill of becoming even more powerful. The authority that came with packing heat was beyond compelling. It wasn't necessarily the idea of overpowering another human being, but more so the quickness and speed of getting away with it and getting one step closer to the exit from my circumstances.

This life of crime wasn't the life I wanted, but it *was* all I knew. When friends and neighbors were going to bed hungry or with holes in their shoes, busting routes kept my family and me from going without too. But still, part of me felt lost, most of the time empty. I knew I was living the definition of stolen identity.

JUST AS EXPECTED, AN EARLY-MORNING KFC employee was prepping for the day with the back door held slightly open by a garbage can. I rushed up to the drive-thru window and pressed my body close against the frame so no one driving from behind the restaurant could see what I was doing.

"Uhh . . . good morning," she said, confused and with a tone of apprehension. "Baby, you're gonna have to go around through the front door, not back here." And just like that, a split second before she finished her sentence, I slid in through the cracked door and pointed a nickel-plated .22 pistol at her ribs.

"Look, lady, don't trip, just give me the fucking money, and I'll get on with it." The nervous twitch tugged at my lip and right eye, giving the effect of a rabid dog's growl. As I barked orders for her to stop stalling and give up the money from the register *that wasn't hers*, I noticed the safe tucked under the counter on the other side of the greasy kitchen floor. I aggressively motioned for her to get down on the ground to open it. Her hesitation triggered my impatience, making my stomach flip. Every second mattered, and the longer it took, the more violent a character I would have to produce. "Hurry up, bitch, before you make me do something to you!" But for anyone who knows me, being violent or actually shooting anyone is something I could never bring myself to do.

Strangely enough, I never even considered wearing a mask like everyone else who knocked over these establishments. In my mind, if you could see me, you could feel me, and what I wanted people to feel was that I was just a good guy doing a bad thing. Because to me, that was the truth. Besides, *this ain't even your money. This shit isn't personal. Who's it really going to hurt anyway?* That was my mentality. That rhetorical question made it possible for me to pull off these capers even when it started to become emotionally difficult.

□ □ □

ON THAT CHILLY FALL OCTOBER morning in 1996, I remember waking up feeling a certain kind of way. Nothing too specific stood out from any other given Monday, but there was *something* there, like a feeling in my gut I just couldn't put my finger on. I was about seventeen and a half, but I can recall being contemplative, asking myself if rapping with my favorite older cousin, Gillie, might be a better way of getting to the finer things I was risking my life for.

Even though we were cousins, Gillie and I had only met a year earlier. I came home from one of my juvenile bits and one day, as these boys were rapping in a cipher, I'm walking and Gil's standing right there. Ciphers were informal circles where everyone spit their hottest bars. As a teenager, I really thought I was going to be a rapper, so I was rapping all the time. As the cipher progressed, the rappers who had the better bars kept going, while everyone else became spectators. This is what happened with me and Gil. After a few rotations, Gil and I were the last two remaining. We get to battling, and Gil bodies me. So much about a battle is watching how the crowd reacts, and it became obvious to admit defeat.

After the battle, I told Gil he was nice and asked for his number, because I related to Dice Raw, a well-respected rapper in Philly who was fucking with the Roots at the time. This was around the time they dropped that *Do You Want More?!!!??!* album. Two days later, I hit Gil on the phone and tell him to come through to Nanny's crib. So he came over to the crib, and as soon as Stevie saw him, he said, "Cousin, what's up?" *Cousin?!* Stevie must've peeped the confused look on my face and explained that we were cousins related by our grandmothers on our mother's side. Now, I imagine some of you reading are probably scratching your heads, asking, *How Wallo ain't know his cousin?* Y'all can live in the same city, but between all the ripping and running I was doing, even the important details of your life can sometimes be missed.

Back in October 1996, I was sitting at the edge of my bed with a rubber-banded knot of hundreds in my hands. I bobbed my head and recited Ice-T's "High Rollers" rap like it was the Ten Commandments: *"Cash flow extreme, dress code supreme, vocabulary obscene, definition: street player, you know who I mean."* I drifted off, envisioning what it would be like to be in a rap group doing our thing. *Yeah, me and Gil, killing it onstage, going on tour, bagging all the baddest hoes; hell yeah, that would be everything!*

For me, music is God, or maybe God is a DJ. When I was that age, music had an answer for everything. Whether it was love, a breakup with your girl, or something to help ignore the bad weather, I always looked to music to push me through. And if I'm keeping it transparent, there's something about the lyrics from some of my favorite groups that would guide many of my most reckless, impulsive moves. It had a way of making my world feel like a movie. It was the score of my harsh reality. Music transformed me from a half-assed menace to a bona fide street demon. On that day, Ice-T was my soundtrack, and I began dreaming about my and Gillie's own lyrics.

I grabbed the backpack on the floor next to me, searching for a pen to start writing a few bars down, but I paused and thought, *Man, who are you fooling? There hasn't been a pen or pad in this bag for the last two school years!* As I looked up and saw my reflection in the cracked mirror on the dresser, I laughed at myself crazy loud, hoping not to wake anyone else up. *There goes the bright lights, the fame, and all the groupie hoes*, I told myself. Mine and my cuzzo's imaginary rap group quickly faded to black because I used my backpack to steal everything you could think of but a pen and/or pad.

The black hooded sweatshirt I wore that morning was my good-luck charm. Although it had a bunch of nasty ketchup stains and smelled musty as fuck, that's the type of griminess that came with the territory. No matter how much name-brand fly shit I had piled up in my closet, a sweatsuit with a hoodie was the stick-up kid's uniform. I wore it with pride, like stripes on a soldier's sleeve. Straight up, I wouldn't give a damn what was on that jawn; I wasn't about to wash any of that good luck off it.

The weeks leading up to that day had been super sweet. I pulled off a few clean, successful routes and didn't have a single hiccup. At times I would find myself being overly sure and shamelessly proud of myself: I went from learning the tricks of the trade from Steve, to now busting routes on my own like a well-oiled machine. I went from being "Steve's little brother" to becoming just "Wallo" not too long after taking my "how to rob a motherfucker" training wheels off.

My smaller yet older brother, Steven, was a master at whatever he put his mind to. He was older by five years, but by how he moved around, you would think he had me beaten by a lifetime. Like my father, Wallace, and Steve's father, Hip, he was dead serious about the hustler's life. Little Steve played no games when it came to getting money and making sure he looked crisp while doing it. Steve's hair was curly like a Puerto Rican's, and his caramel-colored skin made him stand out around everyone. Because of his compact height, we called him "Little Steve." But his aura and energy were way grander than any grown man in the hustler's game I'd ever seen. I wanted to be as smooth as him. His pick-pocket skills were unmatched, immaculate, un-fucking-detectable. He could swipe your wallet from your coat pocket, slip a credit card out, and put it right back in your pocket, all while standing in your face talking to you.

□ □ □

JUST A FEW MORE ROUTES *and I'll be done* was my motto.

On that October day, as I barged into the dirty chicken kitchen, I knew all the thoughts that conflicted with my mission had to be wiped out of my mind. I couldn't be one foot in and one foot out and still make clear decisions. With my borrowed menacing facial expressions, the ones my nervous twitch loaned me, from the corner of my eye I saw a cop car riding slowly behind me.

Be cool, Wallo, I told myself while internally panicking and mapping out my next move.

"Ma'am, is everything okay?" the officer said suspiciously.

"Hey, yeah, everything alright!" I confirmed as I waved him off with my empty left hand, concealing the gun in my right.

The officer pulled off, turning around the drive-thru, but my intuition told me he would be back and was just calling for backup. I slipped past the frantic woman who was now yelling, pissed I couldn't grab the money in time. I slid across the slippery floor as I exited the side door. *Wee-ooh-wee-ooh-wee-ooh.* The sounds of at least three or four cop cars speeding across the main intersection blared in the near distance.

My heart pounding at about a thousand beats per second, I made a sharp left and took off running down the block. More cop cars were going at top speed, running through red lights, headed in my direction. I took the gun out, tossed it under a parked car, did a backspin, and started hauling ass toward Broad Street and Clearfield.

It got to the point where I was running out of steam when I saw my childhood friend's father, Mr. Sammy, a few blocks ahead. Mr. Sammy was a man of the community, held in high esteem. He was waving me down and screaming for me to come his way. Petrified and fearing for my life, I ran toward Mr. Sammy, praying that I wouldn't die.

He grabbed me, put his arms around me, and said, "Listen to me,

Wallo. I don't know what you did, but do what I say so that I can get you through this safely."

My knee-jerk reaction was to say *fuck that* and keep running, but I was tired. My body, my mind, and my soul were all tired. I got on the ground face down with tears in my eyes. Still just blocks away from Nanny's house, I would have done anything to reverse the time and be there with her looking through old photo albums with my dad inside.

1996

DETECTIVE: So you're telling me this is your third or fourth arrest within the last five years?

INMATE PEEPLES: Yeah. Something like that . . . but I was trying to say that every other time I got arrested, they took me down to the juvenile detention center. You do know I'm still a minor, right? What am I doing here?

DETECTIVE: Were you ever arrested before today with possession of a loaded gun?

INMATE PEEPLES: No, never! I wasn't arrested today with a loaded gun, either. I tossed it under the car before 5.0 even got their hands on me. So, what gun? I didn't have one!

COURT OFFICIALS TORE THROUGH LAYERS of my paperwork line by line. Hearing them repeat my own words from the interrogation room felt like an out-of-body experience. *Did I really say that stupid shit?* I asked myself, knowing that I did. It's exactly what Nanny meant when she'd say, "That Steven might be worse out here than you, but he's definitely smarter than you, kiddo. At least he knows how to get himself out of trouble, but you, Wally-O, I don't know what to say about you!"

Being in that dusty, dark, and stale interrogation room forced my mind to run down memory lane, whether I wanted it to or not. I was angry. I rehashed all the fuckups and left turns I made when I should have gone right. Mistakes and cherished moments flashed before my eyes like a life storybook. With every mental page I turned, I questioned why I made the decisions I did and why it was so difficult for me to simply learn from them. *Why didn't I just finish school and stay out of the way?* And then there's the fucked-up night with Baby D and Lil Shooter that quietly haunts me to this day, playing on a loop in my mind while I sit there anxiously waiting for the interrogation. All those memories rushed back to me as I tried madly not to think about the fact that this time, I might be certified and tried as an adult.

After five years of back-and-forth in juvenile detention centers, anyone with a halfway decent brain would think I would have learned my lesson. I tried. I started showing up to school and going to a few classes, which was a lot for someone with a hooky record longer than the books my teachers tried forcing me to read. I was putting in the effort to do right, and it had been almost two years since my last stint at the detention center. I was on my way to becoming a better student, friend, son, and young man, all with my best intentions. I swore to God I would get my shit together as long as no one ever connected me or even so much as talked to me about what had happened the night before between Baby D and Shooter. I was determined to get on a new path. My dedication to change lasted longer than I would have ever imagined, but there I was, dry snitching on myself in an interrogation room, facing my biggest fear: life in an adult prison.

"Mr. Peeples, isn't it true that if it weren't for Mr. Sammy protecting you from your own stupidity, you probably wouldn't be sitting here in this courtroom?" the court counselor urged with her questions. "There was a great possibility of you being shot dead by the police, who, by the way, were only doing their duty and could have ended your life or, God forbid, someone else's, for that matter. Do you have any idea how much worse this could have turned out? There would have been no one to take the blame for that but yourself! Isn't that right, Mr. Peeples?" Her voice drifted off as she spun on her worn-out block-stacked heels. For some reason, I wasn't sure if she was genuinely asking me these long, drawn-out questions to confuse me or if she was just attempting to have me shook, because if it was the latter, it worked.

I looked around the courtroom, hoping to catch a glance from a pair of loving eyes, someone who would give me a look that said, *I got you. Everything's gonna be alright.* But catching their eyes, I saw that even Nanny and my mother lost faith in both me and the system. My family had grown tired of my broken promises and the burden I'd put on them. Somehow, they felt that if I had been sat down behind bars long enough, it would finally do the trick, and I'd come out a better person. But there wasn't any clear rehabilitation for me until I fought for it, and that didn't come until I ran out of patience with myself.

PUBLIC DEFENDER E. GREEN: Your Honor, in a final attempt to recommend that my client Wallace Peeples and the charges brought against him be amendable to the juvenile justice system, I would suggest consideration of the recent psychological examination of Mr. Wallace Peeples which indicates below-average intelligence, auditory memory, and attention span inadequate; reading level corresponds to the 2.7-grade level at the current age of 17. Also noted are six significant signs of personality characteristics consistent with explosiveness, impulsiveness, lack of emotional warmth, a strong need to give the impression of being socially accessible, use of fantasy and avoidance as defense mechanisms, further noting an immature and suspicious individual who may also be experiencing feelings of personal inadequacies and insecurity with disturbed emotional state.

THE COURTROOM FELL SILENT, AND all I could hear was the *tick-tock* of the second hand on the wall clock. The next thing I knew, I was being handcuffed again and escorted out and into the hall leading back to the tombs. "Yo, let me go," I yelled while yanking my arms away from what we used to call "toy cop courtroom security." At that moment, I was completely lost.

"Yo punk ass got a ten to twenty max, and I could make that time real fucked up for you if you don't relax," the officer said with a dirty smirk across his mug.

"Ten to twenty max?" I repeated to myself. "Ten to twenty *what*?"

"Years."

TWO CORRECTIONAL OFFICERS CAME BARGING through the narrow hall where my holding cell was, rattling a couple of heavy brown sacks full of gunmetal chains and cuffs. Inside the sacks were wrist and ankle shackles for my ride to SCI Dallas. I had never been shackled before. Handcuffed, yes, but shackled chain-gang style, never! I tried holding on to the last few minutes I had left of the world I had already grown familiar with. My friends, my family, and my freedom were moments from being snatched from me, and the sound of those shackles clattering together became too hard to ignore. The more I tried to block out what was to come, the louder and closer the noise grew, reminding me that life as I knew it was almost over.

"Peeples," the short, stocky C.O. yelled. I stood quiet and didn't bother to reply. They knew where I was and didn't need me to assist them in strapping me up for the bus ride to hell.

The heavy metal door slammed loudly behind us. There were twelve of us *criminals* ready to be shipped off. All of a sudden, random Bible stories popped in my head—something about the twelve disciples and breaking bread. All I know is that, in that instance, the church seemed to be the only place my mind would drift off to with every step our chain gang took in unison. But I held on to the vision, damn near walking with my eyes closed.

"Wake yo ass up, sweet meat; you're not in juvie camp no more," the other plump correctional officer joked.

"No shit," I mumbled, praying to God that no one heard.

Most of us sat quietly to ourselves on the two-hour-long bus ride to the state prison. Others did a whole lot of shit-talking, cursing, and threatening to do some wild shit. I looked over at the one doing the most trip'n and noticed his cuffs had a black box over them on both his wrists and ankles. I had no idea what that meant, but I figured it meant the motherfucker was nothing to be played with. I found out later that those black boxes were an added layer of protection for some of the worst motherfuckers to be locked up with: the straight-up murderers, who pretty much feared no one. I turned my head away quickly. I tried to refocus my attention and catch a glimpse through the window grates of the world I was leaving behind. But between the grates and the salty tears that started to fill my eyes, I couldn't make out where I was and still could not mentally process where I was going.

Our bus arrived just in time for rec hour, and every cellblock was out in the yard at the same time. There were hundreds of grown-ass men, diesel and cut up like UFC fighters. SCI Dallas is a state penitentiary in Luzerne County, Pennsylvania, about a two-hour drive from North Philly. It houses about two thousand people convicted of crimes, four hundred of whom are serving life sentences. Think about that: For every ten people you encountered in that prison, two were never going home. Shit, as far as the state was concerned, they *were* home. But that was the energy I was around: men who knew where they'd draw their last breath.

And here I was, a scrawny seventeen-year-old kid, about to be locked in a cage with grown-ass men! *Ahhh, shit! What the fuck did I get myself into?* I panicked. There was a huge difference between what I was seeing as a new inmate and what I saw while paying visits to see my step-pops and uncle up here. On visits, I'd go straight to the visiting room, grab a few snacks from the vending machine, play a hand of cards, talk some greasy shit, and I might see twenty other inmates at a time in one spot. But seeing the prison yard from this perspective honestly scared the living shit out of me. I imagined myself getting stomped out violently and immediately thought that I had to find something and someone who could protect me quickly.

The cells I did the fifteen-year bit in for the robbery are the size of a bathroom in a house; imagine an eight-by-ten room. The floors were slimy, cold, and damp, and the air was thick with the gut-punching stench of crusty toe-jammed feet, dirty ass, and who the hell knows what else. If this wasn't the devil's playground, I don't know what is! Your whole life exists in your bathroom. There ain't no living room, ain't no bathroom, no kitchen, none of that. Ain't no basement, ain't no driveway. Two people occupying that space together for years. That's your house. And when I say living in the bathroom, my cell-mate got to take his shit. He is putting the sheet over that joint with that cabinet into the bed and he's shitting and I'm sitting at the table two feet away. He just going to have a mean flush game because in jail you got the power flush so you keep flushing, so it'll downplay the smell.

I've attempted to think of another way to convey what it feels like to live in a cell, but the truth is I'm so institutionalized it's normal to me. When you're in jail, you got to see things from a different lens. It's the only way to survive. If I looked at things from the lens of how things happened outside the wall, I'd have gone crazy because I'd be scared. When you're shook, you're in trouble. And when you're in trouble, the time you do begins to fuck with you.

One thing I knew from the moment the bus pulled up, each of us chained to the other, was that I had no intention of being there any longer than I had to. Without fully understanding my purpose, I knew I had to change my life drastically to get on the right path. I didn't know it then, pulling up to the yard as a terrified teenager, but I would soon begin changing my life. It started with me being the person who motivated anyone who would listen to do just one thing better than they did the day before. It got to the point where my new nickname became "the Happiest Nigga in Prison." And I was okay with that because I wasn't ever looking to earn stripes from a place that had nothing more to offer.

But I didn't get there overnight.

MY FIRST COUPLE OF WEEKS at SCI Dallas were beyond sur-real. I ran into so many homies from around the way and old bunkies from all the years I'd spent in juvie that at times it sort of felt like a neighborhood reunion.

Every time I went out to the yard, you would hear "Aye, yo Wallo" from the other side of it. If we got lucky, we were able to chop it up for a few minutes through the fence and check in and get a temp on each other.

"Yeah, Slim, they gave me life in this motherfucker, but you know, that ain't about nothing. I'll get off on appeal real soon and be back home in a minute." I swear, if I had a dollar for every time I heard that same bullshit line, I could have afforded a big-time mob lawyer to get me up out of there ahead of my time! It was crazy; I saw homies from every corner of the hood up in there, and it sort of felt good to know I had a few cool people just in case I needed to make a move. The only thing was that my young comrades, who were certified as adults, were separated from the old heads until our eighteenth birth-days. It was kind of like they wanted to take the training wheels off before they brought us out of the bubble to fend for ourselves against the real wolves.

Most inmates came from different areas of Pennsylvania: North Philly, South Philly, Pittsburgh, and small towns in between. Ter-ritories were established by city, race, and sexuality. The gay buls had their own little sections. To this day, I still don't know if that was set up to protect them from us or us from them because, as far as I'm concerned, some of the more effeminate-presenting men were ten times more vicious with the knuckle game than straight dudes. If you ever thought you were going to get one off on them because they were *soft*, shit, I promise you had another think coming. Besides, it was an unspoken rule that if you ended up in a scuffle with one of them, it was assumed to be a lover's quarrel, and from then you were viewed as suspect. They didn't call it "the Pink Palace" for nothing. The main lesson learned from the gate was *Mind your fucking business or be prepared to get worked.* Unfortunately, inside the cage, that lesson alone held more weight than any verse from the Quran and the Bible put together. There are some things that took place behind those walls that many would kill over if they were to leak to the outside world—things that could break up families, create deadly rivalries, or worse, like leave you with your head gushing, split down to the white meat with no one willing to help. As curious as I always was about everything and everyone, I knew not to question many of the things I didn't understand or know.

Weeks slowly but surely turned into months, and sooner than later, I was waking up on my eighteenth birthday. "Happy birthday to you," the old, wrinkled, white correctional officer with salt-and-pepper hair hummed. His ass was as happy as a pig in shit as he jiggled his keys to pull me out of the dorm. By that time, I had been alone with my thoughts long enough to think about stupid shit like when you slow the tempo of the song played at weddings, *dun-dun-du-dun*, it somehow sounded strangely similar to the song played at a funeral. *Dun-dun-du-dun!* And on that day, my birthday song was no different. Same melody, but a way different feeling. Unfortunately for me, there wasn't anything fun about waking up to a state guardsman humming "Happy Birthday" to me on the way to my final destination. "Peeples, you're up. Time for you to grow some hair on your chest," he proudly said. It was my eighteenth birthday, and at that moment, I felt I might've been better off dead.

UPSTAIRS, A BUNDLED BEDROLL, A shirt, and prison pants were launched right at my head by an inmate from inside the registration office. Now, I ain't never been the most athletic cat by any means or any measure, but I managed to catch my new uniform and cell bedding right before I embarrassed myself by dropping them on the wet floor.

"Sinclair! Get the fuck out of here," the husky voice of the registration officer yelled.

"What I do, Mrs. Walker?" the inmate in the brown uniform replied like he didn't know.

"Whoa, whoa, whoa, nah, Mrs. Lady, I'm okay, he's cool," I quickly said before she answered him.

"Shut the fuck up, little nigga, and mind your business," Sinclair shot back at me, laughing as he walked out of the office and down the hall. *Ain't this a bitch*, I thought. I wasn't even in the so-called adult prison for longer than an hour and was already getting chumped.

A few other inmates waiting to be checked in laughed while others watched me like a hawk. But one thing I already knew before I got to this level, where the real big dogs were, was that I wasn't made up of nothing tough, and that I had to figure out the mental warfare of this new land as soon as possible.

"Peeples. Come in, take a seat," the registration officer instructed. Mrs. Walker was a white woman with dark eyes. Hoping my innocent deer-in-headlights eyes would get me on her good side, I sat down.

"Peeples, this is your permanent identification. From here on you're inmate DG2670. If you are caught anywhere without your identification, you will be sent to solitary confinement. Do you understand me?" she questioned, without raising her head to look at me.

"Yes," I said and lowered mine.

"Oh, and this section right here is missing," she said, pointing to a fill-in-the-blank area on my inmate profile page. "Where would you like your body sent in case of death?"

Knowing that I was still a minor, she caught the shock on my face and rephrased it. "In case of a medical emergency, who do you want us to contact?"

The reframing did very little to soften the blow of the reality. *I could die in here.* When you're running the streets, no one thinks they could be the ones in a cell, or in a pine box. That night, I cried myself to sleep.

"MAN, IF YOU DON'T GET** the fuck away from me with this bullshit. I told y'all that boy was stupid," I overheard my bunky, Mitch, yell at Ray as I rounded the corner to go back to my cell. Ray was the appointed block messenger, and from the sound of it, Mitch didn't want to hear shit from him or anyone.

Every block had a messenger, someone who would relay messages and warnings and pretty much be the designated middleman for negotiations between different cliques and crews. Usually, this position is predetermined and given to someone who has no business being in jail in the first place. They are often the *square bears* of the real world, most likely related to someone of power behind the wall, or maybe they handled business for someone with street cred on the outside who was strong enough to make things happen behind the wall. Oftentimes, they would be accountants or some type of finance guy who helped wash money for big-time dealers and ended up taking a first-degree misdemeanor charge—or "M1"—for a body they didn't have anything to do with. Either way, they were typically too lame to be a part of any crews putting in work on the blocks, but too crucial to a head honcho to get fucked up like the rest of the squares that got abused and punked for their commissary and whatnot.

By the time I got around to our cell, Ray was already heading back up the tier, shoving what looked like a couple of boxes of Newports into his pants.

"What happened, dog? You got shook down for your 'ports, or what?" I asked Mitch. The next thing I knew, I was flying into my cell wall without any warning.

"I keep telling you to mind your fucking business and stop playing so fucking much, kid!"

I got up from under the sink basin, where Mitch pushed me, holding the back of my aching head. "Hold up, man, what did I do?"

"You talk too fucking much."

What was he talking about?

If I had to bet money on it, I would have never thought it would be me and my bunky getting into it, but there I was, blocking and swinging in my first of a few prison rumbles I had no business being in. We tussled in that tight space, throwing heavy-handed body blows and gripping each other by our stiff brown shirts. Trying our damnedest to not make too much noise, we repeatedly cursed "Fuck you, nigga" through gritted teeth with every punch we landed. One thing was for sure: we both knew that no matter what was happening, neither of us wanted to be dragged to solitary confinement, "the hole," so we fought as quietly as we possibly could.

Mitch was a lot stronger than me and definitely had more experience in throwing hands, so it was pretty easy for him to beat my ass and get out of our scuffle without breaking much of a sweat. I was dazed and curled up like a puffy cheese doodle between the cinder block and our bunk railing. Mitch looked down at me, breathing heavily, with his fists clinched tight like a set of bowling balls. He spat right next to where I lay tucked and curled up.

It all happened so fast; in one breath, he growled like a maniac, "I could kill yo ass, young'n," and in the next, he extended his hand to help me off the floor that he just mopped me with. If you could only imagine the look of confusion that took over my entire grill. Nevertheless, I knew I didn't want any more smoke from him, so I reached my hand to his, hoping it wasn't another setup. Mitch pulled me up to my feet and said, "Straight up, if anyone asks you, let them know I handled my biz in here with you. You hear me?"

"Bet. You got that!"

Out of breath and pacing in four-by-four-foot circles, I paused for a couple seconds to see what Mitch would do next. Mitch changed his white T-shirt, which had been stretched out at the collar. He was as calm as a surgeon who just handled his work with precision. As he stepped onto the tier and blew his signature whistle, I watched as he signaled the homies to meet in the dayroom when the guards were off their post.

Whoosh. That was the sound of my breath being released from my lungs. It was enough to fill a whole air mattress with one go. I didn't realize I was holding my breath in anticipation of Mitch leaving the cell and leaving me the fuck alone. My mind was a complete blur. I had no idea why what just happened took place, but it was sure as hell a wake-up call. It didn't take a genius to understand that whatever this beatdown was for, it was a form of character building and discipline carried out to avoid other, harsher repercussions. The streets, and especially prison protocol, are dysfunctional that way. Even in moments of so-called brotherly love or ghetto attempts at manly education, no matter how simple or detrimental the situation, an ass whoop'n always seemed to be the first plan of action with every lesson you learned.

As I pulled myself together to get ready for chow, Ray stopped right at the doorway of my cell. I balled my fist up at the thought that he might have been sent to finish the job. But Ray laughed. "Chill, Slim, I'm just passing by to relay the message."

"Well, what the fuck is the message?" I groaned.

"Nah, the message isn't for you; I need to relay the message that yo ass got dealt with the way you were supposed to," he said as he looked over his shoulder cautiously.

"Relay the message to who, though, Ray? And for what? What the fuck did I do?" I questioned with deep concern.

"Relax, Slim, it's not that deep. You just caught your first infraction but got lucky; you could've gotten done way greasier."

"Infraction?" I repeated.

"Listen, Slim, it's a free world even in prison. You can do what you want and kick it with who you want, but there are systems in play that keep shit running smooth, and you got to know who, what, and when to speak on certain things." I listened closely, offering nothing more than a look of sheer confusion. Ray let out a deep sigh. "Look. Word is you told one of the Puerto Rican niggas how much the smokes and smut mags were going for on our side of the fence. That's the infraction! Not minding your business blew the lid off the extra points we were stacking on top of everything. It fucked us up in the marketplace a little bit. You gotta understand, there's a really intricate web of prison economy we must keep in order to stay above the bullshit, Wallo. This type of slipup can fuck around and cost somebody their life! You got to learn to listen fast and talk slow."

In that instance, I remembered I had been shooting the shit with one of the new guys and told him who and where he could cop all the good shit from. Shit, I just thought I was looking out for everybody. José gets his nicotine fix and a good time with *Black Tail* pics, and Mitch gets to profit off all of it. That would be a win-win situation, as far as I was concerned.

"You're not a hustler, Slim, you a petty thief! You got lucky to have your pops and a few comrades up here to look out for you, or you would have got poked up in more ways than one for the shit you pulled, you heard me? This shit ain't a game, Wallo. Half these cats are doing life in the Palace, and it ain't shit sweet about it. There's a pecking order up in here, and you're at the bottom of it. A thief ain't nothing more than one notch above a pedophile and a woman beater behind these gray walls. You never put in any real work; you're just a taker, and that don't give you no stripes as a man when it boils down to it," Ray said firmly. That was the first time I thought of it in that way, the first time I felt sick to my stomach with shame.

"Good looking, Ray," I said, nodding.

"Don't thank me," he responded. "Just stay the fuck out of the way. Don't become some booty bandit's food cause your lips too loose."

From that point on, I told myself I would act as dumb as they come. I would go on about my time like I don't know nothing about nothing. From that day on, I would play as green as a frog's skin about everything, and no one would think to ask me for shit or have any expectations of me. Just call me Kermit and leave my goofy green ass alone.

ABOUT A YEAR OR TWO into my time in Dallas, I was in the yard one afternoon and I overheard this dispute between buls from different parts of Philly. One of them had a drug package in, and the other found out. As they were arguing, they walked into the area where the weightlifting equipment was held.

"Motherfucker, stop. I told you!"

The next thing I saw was the bul from South Philly falling over and the bul from North Philly bashing his skull in with a ten-pound weight with so much force that the blood shooting out of his head was like oil was struck—and what terrified me more was the fact that the bul from South Philly was still fighting, even with the blood loss. Though there were two guards on their post in the watchtowers, they were about 300 feet away. And while that's not a great amount of distance, by the time the guards intervened, the bul from North Philly had already hit South Philly ten or fifteen times. All of this transpired in a matter of minutes. For the two buls beefing, both of them had life sentences, so they were literally fighting for their lives.

Despite that incident, contrary to what many people may believe and how it's portrayed in television and movies, prison is one of the most respectful places I've ever been in my life. And I'm going to tell you why: because the smallest little thing could ignite a war, and tensions are so high, everyone prioritizes their safety and survival. Especially when you know you have a life beyond the cell.

THE AIR AND TENSION IN the chow hall were so thick that it would take one of those old turkey handsaws that country folk used to tuck in their kitchen junk drawer to cut through it. Of course, it was always possible to get shanked with a filed-down pipe or cracked upside the head with a rock in a sock down at the chow hall, and today, I worried it might be my turn. To be honest, before this stupid-ass mistake I made, I could say with a straight face that I didn't necessarily fear for my life on a regular basis as most of the other young buls did. Sure, there was always the chance of some unnatural, ungodly act looming over us like clouds made of mud water and savage storms. Especially when it came time to visit the shower stalls, a young tender like me could have easily been made a victim. But those were one-offs, and I did everything in my power to avoid slipping into those sticky situations. Even if that meant washing my armpits and corn chip–smelling feet in the cell sink and skipping out on a couple days of showers from time to time.

There wasn't an eye that didn't look over at me as I crossed the battleground known as the chow hall. I hunched my shoulders as I remembered that the ass whip'n I just took was kind of a consideration hall pass since they allowed my own bunky to discipline me for what I still felt was a minor misunderstanding. It was showtime, and my audience was a cafeteria full of men who would happily beat the brakes off me. So, my walk became a bit more staggered, I started dragging my left leg just a little, and I tucked my tongue into the side of my cheek, holding my face with my hands so it looked like I really got my ass beat.

"Peeples!" I jumped at the sound of C.O. Cole shouting my name from the other side of the cafeteria. This motherfucker was one of the sickest, most vicious guards in the institution. Nobody fucked with him, not even the most thoroughbred murderers. "Cold Blooded" was the name we quietly used for him—quietly, because we never dared speak that name above a whisper. It was like saying Candyman's name five times in the mirror. It was so bad that if someone even hinted that Cold Blooded was on the hunt, you'd know it was time to put yourself on voluntary time-out, no questions asked. I'm telling you this six-five ogre didn't give a fuck; and abusing you before writing you up to do eighteen months or longer in the hole was one of his favorite sports.

That only came second to getting his dick sucked by a peon who was scared to death of extended periods of isolation. He was psychotic and calling me out in front of everyone was the start of the bullshit mind games he'd liked to play with us prisoners just for fun.

Almost forgetting I was supposed to be injured badly, my head whipped around so fast toward the giant wildebeest that I almost caught a crick in my neck, triggering an actual injury. My body stood frozen, and my feet began to feel like I was drowning in quicksand. There had to be at least fifty of us cons in that section of the chow hall, but right then and there, it was only us. Me and Cold Blooded locked eye-to-eye as everyone watched.

"Boy, what the fuck is wrong with you?" he said as he bulldozed his way in my direction, parting the chow line like Moses did the Red Sea.

It was always crazy how some Bible story would surface in my mind from Sunday school at the strangest times, like when I thought I would either get mud-stomped or, worse, die. I guess that's one of the effects of having what they call a "praying grandma" because, in times of uncertainty, there was nothing like a vision of God coming to protect your stupid ass. I promise, if I didn't latch on to some strong memory at that very moment, I would have felled the fuck out like a drama queen, and there is no coming back from some bitch-ass shit like that.

C.O. Cole recklessly pressed up against my face, ribs, thighs, and back with his billy club, poking around possible sore areas to see what parts hurt enough to make me fess up to an earlier square-up. "I said, what the fuck happened to you, Peeples?" This time, he looked around the chow hall for a guilty look or facial expression or maybe to see if anyone's knuckles would show any signs of a fight or bruising. According to legend, there's nothing better than being able to rough off at least two cons for the price of one when it came to him.

If I even blinked my eye in the wrong direction, I would have been labeled a snitch. I looked across the sea of hard-faced inmates waiting eagerly for me to slip, and I decided I'd rather spend the next eighteen months in the hole than be stamped as the cellblock thief and now, a snitch. Fuck, I had to pick the best of two poisons, and being called a rat was never going to be an option.

"Chill, Cold . . ." I caught myself before calling him our pet name for him. "Ain't nothing happened, C.O. Cole. For real. I was just on my top bunk dreaming about one of the baddest bitches in the whole city that I left by herself. Shit, you know there was a party in my pocket, dick hard as a rocket. Next thing you know, I was turning over to get on top of that warm silky bitch, and *BAM*, my dumb ass fell so hard from that top bunk it was like a dope fiend getting bounced out of heaven. Real rap, I fucked my whole shit up, Cole."

Mitch and a few other cats in his crew were watching the whole thing go down from the table right behind me. I looked over my shoulder quickly to see if they heard me copping pleas and make sure they knew I held it down for the homies. Mistake number three. First was thinking I was Bob Barker on *The Price Is Right*. Second was putting on a show for the whole block to see, and third was making eye contact with the homies, who didn't even try to keep their composure. The whole table, including Mitch, couldn't help but let out a gut-roaring laugh. That shit set Cold Blooded smooth off, and as soon as I turned my head back to look at C.O. Cole, my face was being introduced to his elbow. *Wham!*

Now, how the hell did I go from living a halfway-decent existence (compared to the nightmares of others) in one of the worst prisons outside Philly to getting fucked up twice in one afternoon? *This shit is silly!* I thought to myself. But getting whooped by just one man and sent to the hole while everyone forgets about my infraction was the better hand being dealt.

In my three years in the Palace, I witnessed some of the most thorough men come out of the hole totally different from how they went in. I'm talking about indescribable physical and psychological changes to guys who were once beasts among men. There is something about complete isolation, where your only outside source of communication is the nightly blood-curdling screams and the sounds of men's skulls banging voluntarily against paint-chipped walls, that can make you lose your marbles for good. In the hole, you tend to create mind-shattering stories produced by the soundtrack of the wild yells from men stripped naked in boxes just a few feet away from yours. It is a hellish place where the only friends you are able to entertain are the bedbugs that rip your skin to shreds if you're there long enough to learn when to ignore or when to enjoy their presence.

And yet, I still chose the hole over the idea of being labeled a rat, an infraction that no one will ever forgive or forget.

Cold Blooded immediately went to work on me, dragging my still scrawny body out of the cafeteria and slamming me into a holding cell that was usually used when someone was reported 5150, the code for crazy. You couldn't pay me to fight back, talk smack, or show even the slightest sign of resistance, even though I could have sworn that made him even more violent and angry. He wanted me to engage in some action that I was not prepared to give.

There was no reason for C.O. Cole to be so amped up, with the exception that he loved this type of aggressive prison foreplay shit with a passion. "Strip down, motherfucker! I don't want to see a god-damned thing but your bare-naked ass and the lint from up under them little bitch-made balls, loser."

"Whoa, whoa, whoa," I said at a volume much louder and more disrespectful than what I would have wanted to address him with. Still, in my defense, I was frantically trying to gain control of my senses before the muted chokehold of anxiety overtook me and made it impossible to even hear anything demanded by this three-hundred-pound creature of death.

Wham! Another elbow to my face. At this point, I was ready to get it on and fight for my life before giving in to any of his unlawful requests in this soundproof room.

"Why are you fucking with me, Cole? I didn't do shit, I told you that."

Wham! Another elbow, followed by another one. All these gut and rib shots in a row had me folded over, struggling to keep my balance and dry heaving spit and puke from my empty stomach. This went on for what felt like hours before the sound of keys jingling in the holding cell's door caught us both off guard.

C.O. Walker, the intake C.O., pulled the cell door open and asked if Sergeant Slaughter, another nickname for C.O. Cole, needed any help. I couldn't believe this bitch would be so foul to want to join him in taking the last bits of my innocence from me.

"You grimy, fat bitch," I spat as quickly as the thought sprang up about how I would repay her raggedy ass for her unwelcome visit. C.O. Cole smirked and adjusted his belt, bobbing his head from left to right, cracking his neck as loud as a pack of lit Fourth of July firecrackers.

"I said . . . can I help you?" C.O. Walker repeated, only this time, it had a much harsher tone and sternness directed at Cold Blooded, which was unexpected. It was clear as day that she opposed taking part in the filth and vicious type of time C.O. Cole was on and was actually there to rescue me—something that almost never occurs to anyone serving time in state penitentiaries.

I was wrong about C.O. Walker, and probably as I had been about the intentions of some women who came into my life and tried to help me out before her. At that moment, I wanted to make sure that one day she would see me through a different lens, not as the coward and thief I was, standing there with no direction.

Cold Blooded stepped to the side, as cool as a breeze, and it was almost like he was a totally different person. He walked past C.O. Walker without saying a word, making sure not to bump her on his way out with his wide-set Donkey Kong shoulders.

"Alright, let's go, Peeples. Back to your cell!"

I nodded, placed my hands behind my back, and lowered my head. As we stepped out of the doorway, C.O. Walker grabbed my arm to lead the way back to my tier. I was sure that saying thank you wasn't a fitting gesture, but I raised my head anyway to see if she could tell how grateful I was.

Then, reality set in when I looked up and saw Ray, the messenger, just a few feet ahead, scoping out the scene as he usually did. It was safe to assume that Ray had way more pull than I thought and that his muscle on the block was the big-boss-hog C.O. Walker, who somehow had the power to save our Black asses or leave us for dead.

HIGHER LEARNING

COUNTLESS LIES HAVE BEEN TOLD to me throughout my life, many of which were told by the very people I looked up to: the hood heroes, the men who spent time behind the same bars I'd spent time behind. After years of incarceration, these delusional men came right back to the hood and told stories made up of more myth and bullshit than the ones in children's books with three-headed dragons and purple unicorns. The community always welcomed most of these men back home with open arms. We even celebrated their return regardless of what they went in for. Yet most of them had nothing to offer us young and impressionable men but more lies and deception.

"Nah, you're good, young'n. They can't give you no real time until you're grown and putting in some real work. You'll be straight if you ain't robbing no banks or blowing nobody's head off."

That was just one of the lies I was told that made me believe I had the luxury to keep fucking around. I thought I was too young and too smooth to serve sentences in the double digits with lifelong criminals. I hadn't realized I was quickly becoming one of them, route by route. My long list of arrests, dating back to just days after my eleventh birthday, set the stage for my grand entry into a miserable existence that I wasn't mentally prepared for.

My ignorance, half taught and half forced, swiftly caught up to me, and what I once thought was child's play led me right down the path to becoming a certified adult surrounded by men who didn't give a fuck about how old I was or how petty my crimes were. Behind those bars, you were either about that life or you weren't, and if you weren't, you better make sure you know how to play the game like your life depends on it.

Unlike juvie, there were no horseback rides or camping excursions in hopes of helping socialize you and to build trust and self-esteem. In the penitentiary, there was none of that. Although I didn't realize it while in the juvenile detention system, the programs they offered us on rare occasions and simply being around my peers made that time a cakewalk compared to any day in prison. I had taken things for granted and instantly regretted every minute of it the moment I was certified. Somehow, I got caught up in the idea that I had already been through it all, and if I eventually went to prison, I could basically do it with my eyes closed. I'm not sure words could ever describe how wrong I was!

Weekend passes were also a thing in juvie that I didn't realize were the ultimate privilege. I could bus myself home for the weekend and back to the campus before curfew as long as I stayed out of trouble. That privilege was forever stripped from me the moment I went behind the forty-foot concrete wall that surrounded SCI Dallas. No one tells you about lockdown and living in a cell for "twenty-three and one"—that's twenty-three hours alone in a six-by-six cell with nothing but your own voice in your head and the screams of other men who have already gone mad. There is no escaping the thoughts that weave in and out of your mind like a slithering snake filled with deadly venom. Some of the deepest, darkest thoughts find ways to poison every inch of your being to the point where you become your own worst enemy. Your only hope for solace is the one hour granted to you to shower or use the phone if allowed to. Many times we weren't, and even when we could, what could we possibly have to share with the person on the other end of the line but lies and deception so they wouldn't worry? Just like the old heads.

From my top bunk fitted with a vinyl one-inch-thick mattress and sheet that felt like gritty sandpaper, I spent years revisiting the pain and regret of not learning my lesson before getting shipped to a place where pity and remorse were kept quieter than most secrets. It is a place where you are some deranged man's food if frailty is smelled on you. I used the books I pretended to read as shields to protect me from being seen with the tears that flooded my face daily.

During booking, they ask you four questions four different times: Have you ever been under mental health care? What medication, if any, do you take? Are you under medical supervision for mental health? How often, if ever, do you have suicidal thoughts? Even the sanest of men will feel the gravity of those questions pulling at their mental health triggers. *If I wasn't suicidal then, how long would it be before I become that?* Those were the types of questions I asked myself through the soul-snatching intake process. And that was the question I asked myself several times after, repeatedly questioning my stability while at times feeling my mind slip away from me.

Self-inflicted insanity was the only clear way to make it through some of the most treacherous days you probably could never imagine, days where you would wish you didn't have some of your natural-born senses. Not even through blindness can you unsee the thick, purple-colored blood oozing from a man's skull. You can't block the nauseating stench of a crazed inmate rocket-launching a milk carton filled with bubbling, stewed shit into someone's cell. And you could never forget the sound of sharpened steel slicing in and out of someone's neck and collarbone. There's nothing quite like the gushing sound of blood from a hot spike piercing through the jugular of a man, now gasping for his last breaths.

Trying to remain sane in the most insane places was begging for a mental fracture that could never be repaired. I quickly learned that prison is similar to golf in that it is strictly a game of opposites—except there aren't any lush green acres of grass or caddies to help carry the weight and make game-changing decisions. One thing I always had to remember is that behind the wall, when things appeared too right, they would often go far left, and getting too comfortable could be a fatal flaw. You had to always keep your head on a swivel at all times because one day you were someone's best friend, and the next you were their mortal enemy, being stared down and preyed on.

PHONE TIME WAS ANOTHER ROLL of the dice. You never knew what someone had going on in their life at the times you were able to get through. People said they would hold you down, but sooner than later, most of them forgot about you.

"I don't give a fuck what none of these motherfuckers got to say; you're my baby, Wallo," Brenda said seductively on the other end of the phone. Big-Booty Brenda was my girlfriend back in the real world. Well, actually, she wasn't really my girl-girl; she was my piece. My favorite one at that. I couldn't claim her out loud on the front streets, but we did everything and anything you could imagine a couple would do to each other and for each other every time we'd meet. Brenda was an older woman—I was only thirteen when we met—who took pleasure in grooming young cats like me—cats that had considerable potential to make some noise and bring back loads of money someday. She had an eye for hood stars and future big-time players, and she knew exactly when and how to swoop in and put you onto the game before someone else did.

"Yeah, but check this out, Brenda; that was cute and all that when we were both outside and could move how we chose to, but now I'm stuck in here with your real man, and I don't need that kind of action while I'm doing this time," I said in a low but stern tone.

"Oh, I'm just Brenda now, huh? I wasn't Brenda when you were running in and out of my house, eating, drinking, and getting fucked like the man I thought you were! It was *baby this* and *baby that*. Now you're in a little jam, and you forget who the fuck put your nut ass onto all this good shit? Well, I hope those little bum bitches you keep calling out here trying to line up got something to put on your books because I sure the fuck won't. You're on your own," she said, laughing as she knew she had me by the balls.

"Now, hold up, you said you got me for life, remember? You know I can't be phone bone'n on the line with you up in here. Why the fuck are you trying to give me a hard time? You know what you mean to me; you're my bitch for real. Let's not ever get that shit twisted." She loved it when I talked greasy to her. That was part of my Philadelphia Slim image that she helped groom.

"Oh, that's what I thought! And you better not forget that 'cause if I hear about one more of these little hoes talking about you putting them on your visitation list, we gonna have a problem," she said, only half-jokingly.

"Yeah, okay B, shut yo ass up and just make sure you put something on my account today, or I'll fuck around and miss the store until next week. You know my skinny-ass ribs are already touching, so you better make sure your favorite nigga gets to eat."

We hung up without exchanging a single word of encouragement, not one *I love you*, nothing that would come from a healthy, loving relationship. None of that was ever considered because we didn't come from that. Those were the micro-moments of love shared only between people brought up in healthy, worthy, and unbroken homes. We were none of those things. She was a gangsta, a pimp, a lady of the night, and I was her plaything, a disciple of her sermons, and a do-boy that did whatever she instructed because her hand called for it.

Talking to Brenda was like time-traveling back to when I was young, dumb, and free, with the type of willful ignorance that seemed to chase away time, rules, laws, and boundaries. At times, I wasn't sure who was running the most game, her or me. That bitch always knew the right thing to say, even when she was dead-ass wrong. She had a way with words; she was slick and quick-witted, and not too much got past her. But it was her body that caught my eye the first time I laid eyes on her. She was stacked like a track and field runner who ate one too many slices of red velvet. She had just the right amount of muscle tone yet also juicy, jiggling thickness. Her thighs were like pillows. Smooth as satin. I can't even lie; she turned me all the way the fuck out like she was the daughter of Satan!

I could remember as clear as day seeing Brenda slide through the neighborhood in her ivory-white Mercedes-Benz with chinchilla fur trim and matching driving gloves in the winter. She was a dope dealer's dream girl. Everything about her, from head to toe, was exclusive because if there was one thing about her, she always had money to burn. There weren't too many females from our side of Philly that had it made the way she did. Of course, there were the around-the-way fly girls who could finesse some fly shit from the dope boys like a couple pairs of shoes and a Coach or Gucci bag here and there. But those luxury pieces didn't come easy like they did for Brenda.

Those girls actually had work to do. They couldn't just kick their feet up, collect their trinkets, and be cute. Nah, they had to get their asses up and bust moves up and down 95 South like mules and make some things happen for their dealer daddies before they could even think about flipping through a fashion catalog. Those were the girls who were either getting robbed by their sidepiece boyfriends, the ones who had time to give them a little attention, or they were getting knocked by the feds for doing too much and running their mouths, but either way, they were dispensable no matter how fly they were. Not Brenda, though. She was one of one and nothing like them!

One cold November night, between the shadows of the dingy streetlamps and the flickering fluorescent corner-store lights, Brenda double-parked her car, signaling with her hazards on as if she were waiting for someone or something to pull up on her. I knew it was her by the sparkling-clean beams bouncing off her rims like the light glistening from a chandelier. Those shits were always clean like we didn't live in a city with four seasons leaving trails of black ice and snow from just a couple nights ago. Shorty was just impeccable with how she handled her handle. I stood there trying not to look suspicious, eating a bag of Doritos and sipping an orange soda, admiring how rich she always looked, like she didn't belong there. I couldn't help but stare, picturing myself driving that car with the seat reclined while bumping me and my cousin Gillie's music through the system. I could just imagine how hard they would be sweating me pulling up in a Big Body Benz. But that vision was quickly dissolved by the sound of a high-pitched beep coming from Brenda's pager through her window. I noticed she kept the windows cracked, which meant she could afford to have the heat turned up high enough for her to let in some crisp air and not have to worry about wasting gas. *Damn, this bitch is bad*, I thought to myself.

Another moment passed by, and her pager went off again. I could see her looking around for something between the dashboard and the passenger seat. When she looked up and out the window, we caught each other's eyes, and I damn near choked. I tried to look away quickly so she didn't think I was up to something, but she made sure I knew she saw me looking.

"Aye, little man, come here; let me give you something to do," she said while letting down her button-powered window. I looked around, confused, pointing to myself. "Yeah, you come get this bread," she yelled.

"Little man?" I shot back. I always had a thing for being called anything that made me seem smaller or less capable than how I felt.

She sucked her teeth and said, "Boy, please, forget it, I'll do it myself." As soon as she went to get out of her car, I sprinted and was already leaning at the passenger-side window, waiting for her to tell me what she wanted.

"Hey, what's your name? Since you clearly don't like to be called 'Little Man,' " she said with a slight smile.

"Wallo," I said, struggling to deepen my voice.

"Wallo? What kind of name is that?"

"It's short for 'Wallace Rocks a Lot of Polo,' " I said, making that shit up off the top of my head.

"Oh okay, Wallo, open your hand," she said while extending hers. "Take this beeper and a couple dollars and see if you can get the corner store to give you some change. When the beeper goes off from a 704 area code, use the change to call them back from that pay phone and tell them you'll be waiting for them here to drop off the work."

"Wait, huh?" I asked, trying to process what she just said.

"Come on, Wallo, this shit is basic; you heard what I said!" I did, but I was confused and shook into a daze.

"I just saw you pull out that big-block cell phone from underneath the passenger seat; why won't you just use that instead?" I questioned.

She shook her head and sucked her teeth again, then said, "You got a lot to learn, Little Man," and grabbed the gear shift like she was about to pull off and leave me for dead.

I leaned back with a snarl on my face. "Yo, it's Wallo, and why the fuck are you even asking me to do this shit if I'm so little? Shit, I don't even know you like that, Ms. Whatever-Your-Name-Is."

She laughed half-heartedly and said, "You're right, Wallo, my bad. But I know your people, and I've heard some big-time-player shit about your dad. I'm just looking out for you and helping you a little bit 'cause I hear you have some pretty big shoes to fill."

It didn't take much more for me to hop right on board. If there is one thing about Philly, word gets around easily. There isn't too much shit that stays low around here. Good, bad, or indifferent, it didn't matter. If you had a dollar in your pocket or you were making a little noise anywhere from here to downtown, a word about where you got it or how loud it was would get out.

My father's name rang bells long enough for the generations after him to know at least a story or two about him. Just the mention of his name would have me jumping through hoops like a two-bit fool. There wasn't anyone I looked up to more than the legend of my pop dukes.

Brenda definitely knew exactly what she was doing when she mentioned my pedigree. And if she didn't know right then, she found out soon enough because I quickly became her most dedicated soldier. I had a point to prove and a heavy chip on my shoulder.

□ □ □

AFTER HANGING UP WITH BRENDA I paused, letting out a deep exhale before walking back to my cell. My head felt heavy, hanging over my slumping shoulders. Anyone with a decent eye could tell I was in a funk because I wasn't my usual hyperactive self after talking my shit on the phone.

Big June, one of the homies from the block, yelled across the room, "Look at this limp noodle, got caught up fantasy-mac'n on the jack; now he can't hold his neck up." My eyes darted across the room, laser-beaming a hole into him. My blood was already boiling, and my heart was racing like a cokehead. I hadn't always been so quick to anger, but as time passed, living in the dirty dungeon that was now my home, I began to feel more and more like a targeted victim.

"Yo, June, mind your fucking business," I yelled back at him. And just like that, I saw a light flicker in him. It was as if he'd been waiting for any chance he got to flip on me. Something so petty, so insignificant, some shit he started was all it took to warrant a beef between him and me if the opportunity was presented.

Luckily, two guards were walking the perimeter when shit was about to pop off. No one was stupid enough to set it off with the law around unless there was something major taking place and you wanted to escape by being put in the hole. It wasn't that serious for either of us, but it was definitely noted that Big June wanted an issue with me and that it would soon come to a head. Just not at that moment.

Back in my cell, I just wanted to be alone. There were days I'd skip going out to the yard or the dayroom just to be alone with my thoughts. Peace and quiet were something money couldn't buy, so on the rare occasion my bunky wasn't around, I would take advantage of the time and dig through the crates of my mind. Who am I kidding? Most of the time, when I got the cell to myself, I would have party time with a smut mag and a moistened, handmade fifi bag, but this time wasn't one of them. And maybe Big June was right. I was fantasy-mac'n on the line, and it got me deep into my feelings, something that is never supposed to happen.

The objective of fantasy-mac'n is to sell dreams, not buy them. It gets to the point sometimes where the mac'n gets so good you start to believe your own bullshit. Every man behind bars has a story to tell, but it's the real fantasy-macs who can sell water to a whale. As far as I knew, some big-time macs had up to twenty women at a time believing they were coming home in a few months tops and going to lay them out with houses, diamonds, and furs as long as they kept it tight out there and held them down. Most of them were facing twenty to life, but the sweet sound of an appeal kept these women strung out on every word, and believe it or not, it kept a gang of fantasy-macs' commissaries filled.

"Aye, man, don't trip about that bullshit, you heard?"

I jolted as I heard Mitch's voice say that while standing in front of our cell, joking. I sat up on my bunk, looking at him like I didn't know what he was talking about.

"What you mean? Trip'n on what?"

"They told me you and Big June were about to bump heads a couple minutes ago and that you've been hiding in your bunk like a little hoe," he said, laughing. I laughed too.

"Nah, I was just chill'n, thinking about some things, that's all, man," I said.

"Oh, alright, you know if shit gets too crazy I got you," Mitch said as he walked away.

"Yeah, I'm cool though, real shit," I replied, pretending to be unfazed.

Actually, I wasn't fazed about Big June at all, not at that moment, because I had gone so far down memory lane that I almost forgot where I was laying. It couldn't have been more than twenty minutes that my mind had drifted off—twenty minutes of false freedom to let my mind roam.

It took everything in me not to allow sheer panic to set in. I jumped off my bunk and splashed water on my face from the rusted steel basin. This was the moment I decided to pick up a pen and start writing my "Letters to Freedom." I knew there would be no other way for me to get through this bid without completely losing it.

DEAR FREEDOM,

I miss you! I wanted to start by letting you know how much before moving on. I miss you more than anything in this world. I know I haven't written you in a while. I guess I grew tired of begging for your return. There are lots of things I've grown tired of since I've been away from you.

I'm tired of these walls closing in on me. I'm tired of eating the same dry, bland food. I'm tired of niggas begging for soups, jack mack, or anything to eat in one breath and in the next breath acting like they were some kind of kingpin running shit in the outside world. I'm tired of hearing the bullshit being spewed over the phone by men who haven't spent a second of their time trying to figure out how they're going to make it out of here but want to demand to know where their women have been and with who—as if those women don't have a life and kids to take care of without their men behind bars.

I'm tired of seeing men use up their time playing board games and not utilizing it to upgrade their way of thinking. I'm tired of being the only one in the law library, yet when these cats come back from failed parole hearings, they go right back to shit-talking the system.

When it comes to understanding how the law works, a majority of the dudes are too proud, which is to say they are really too afraid, to admit they don't know as much as they try to make everyone else believe. Many of us confuse breaking the law with knowing it, and because so many of us are distrustful of the system and its tactics, learning all the complicated ins and out of this shit takes more time than a lot of us want to give.

Accustomed to looking for the quickest route to get the highest return, a lot of people at SCI Dallas feel like reading all those law books requires an optimistic or even delusional outlook on a future that isn't guaranteed. So much of what governs life in prison are the things that are tangible—the things that you can touch, taste, smell, hear, and see. Surviving prison requires faith, and by the time many of us arrived here, our faith in anything we couldn't see didn't exist.

At some point, we all have to take accountability and devise a plan for how we want our lives to be going forward. It took me a long time to get to this point, and I know I have a long way to go, but I honestly got tired of seeing those same traits in me, and I just had to do something about it.

The good news is, I took my GED! That shit was hard, but I put all my time and energy into studying and staying focused. Things can really change when you put your mind to it. Now let's just hope I passed it.

By the way, I'm up for my first parole meeting. I refuse to get my hopes up. Since I've been here, I've never seen anyone hit a home run their first time up at bat. But I'm taking this as a practice run, just like I did all the GED prep exams. I had to fail a few times to knock it out of the park.

I'm ready for you, Freedom! You're more than my girl: you're my wife, my life. And when I make it back to you, I promise I'll never betray you again! Until then . . . I'm gone.

Respect and Love,

Wallo

THE MORNING COUNT SEEMED TO have come a little early today. The usual time would be between 5:45 and 6:00 AM, depending on whether or not the C.O.s felt like being dicks and waking us up extra early just because. The good thing was I had already been awake for a while. I was up the last few nights thinking about the things I needed to get done during the next couple of weeks to prepare myself to sit in front of the parole board.

I was always an early bird, so waking up for count wasn't as difficult for me as it was for so many others. No matter how long or short their stay, the morning count always seemed to come as a surprise to them. It wasn't like you couldn't lay back down and go back to sleep if you wanted to. I mean, unless you had a job or didn't want to miss morning chow.

For some, those early-morning counts were torturous. I mean, some cats hated it enough to risk being put in the hole just for not standing for the count like we were supposed to. It was a basic drill: Be up and standing at your cell door when the guards come by to check that you didn't break out the night before, and that was all. I actually made a game out of it where I would line my boots up on the floor to see if one day I could jump down off my bunk and land right in them.

As goofy as that may sound, it was a teeny moment of fun squeezed into my day before the reality of living in a human cage sunk into my head every morning. Truth is, I wasn't the only one awake and alert. But the reason why others were was to be ready to mix it up, a.k.a. rumble in your cell if, by chance, anyone popped your cell lock and wanted to fuck them or their cellmate up. As a matter of fact, there have been times when an inmate even slept with their boots on and a long, chiseled samurai sword made of steel that they ripped from their metal-framed bunk taped to their thigh. In prison, you learn to stay ready so you never have to get ready.

That particular morning, I felt energized and ready to tackle the day ahead. It's rare to feel that way when you're stuck behind bars with murderers and God knows who else. However, I had been optimistic about the life transition and journey I was ready to go on since I'd signed up to get my general education diploma. I know that to a lot of people, a GED isn't worth the paper it is printed on, but it meant a lot to me—a whole lot, actually. I never spent much time in real school when I was free. I started running the streets and going buck wild by the age of nine and started my long list of arrests just after I turned eleven. You could only imagine how far behind I was from the average student on the days I *did* attend.

My records from the juvenile detention centers and psych reports all had varying scores for my education level and intelligence. A few of them scored me at an average grade level or more for reading, while other reports, more detailed, scored me much further below with a reading level of third grade when I should have been in ninth. I saw one report where the doctor assessing me also attached a long, drawn-out response to the assessment takers before him and commented on their lack of care and professionalism in my previous assessments. It was his professional opinion that their reporting was reckless and a liable cause for my subpar level of basic education and literacy at my age.

I was always torn between believing the reports that marked me as incapable of learning, and the psych reports that suggested I had an actual learning disability. Either way, I never allowed myself to be suckered into what others believed of me. I knew that whatever I set my mind to, I would achieve. Even if I was on the lower end of the spectrum when I decided I was going to study to pass my GED, I did just that: I locked in, got laser-focused on my work, and blocked out as much of the noise and distractions from other inmates as I could.

Working toward my high school diploma lit a fire under me. It was something I needed to accomplish to feel worthy. I needed to prove I wasn't dumb or slow or unable to learn, and I proved that by putting my head down and pushing forward even when things got frustrating and difficult. Whatever the feeling was that came over me after getting my passing scores from the practice tests changed how I felt about the world, my conditions, my status as a prisoner, and challenged the low self-esteem and negative feelings I had about myself. That's just how my brain has always worked. I'm either hyper-focused on whatever the circumstance or mission is, or I'm not interested at all. My thoughts are very black-and-white. No grays. No middle ground. I'm the go-hard or go-home type. And now, after this milestone, I'd be ready to do both. Go Hard and Go Home!

Mitch was slower to stand for the count in the morning. He wasn't as bad as other cellies I've had or heard about, but he wasn't the biggest fan of the late nights and early mornings. On days when I woke up in hyper mode, I had to learn to control my readiness to start talking about whatever thoughts came up when we should have been asleep. It was almost like I was being held hostage in my already caged cell until Mitch warmed up to the day and was ready to talk.

I stood up, boots on, with the idea that I would be hitting up the law library as soon as I was done with chow. I glanced through our cell door, and something caught my eye down on the tier below us. *What the fuck is that?* I thought to myself while looking back over my shoulder to see if Mitch was ready for conversation. He was sitting at the edge of his bunk, holding his head in his hands, trying to slowly come out of sleep. I looked back down at the tier below us, seeing a cell sealed off with yellow caution tape. I could hear the sound of keys jingling and figured it was Cold Blooded by the sound of his beastly walk.

Mitch stood up, and I quietly said, "Yo," and pointed downstairs to subtly alert him to what I saw.

"What the fuck?" Mitch said at a much louder volume.

Just then, Cold Blooded walked by, saying, "It should have been one of your asses," laughing as he finished his head count on our tier.

Early mornings were always the best time to get the lowdown on what happened the night before, whether it was something that took place inside the prison walls or out in the hood. It didn't matter; if someone within a hundred miles of Philly had any kind of name worth bringing up, you would know by sunup exactly what they had going on. It could be as simple as one of the homies from around the way traded in their old whip for a new Benz, or they copped a new chain or watch, maybe they stabbed someone and went on a high-speed chase—the morning news brewed overnight was delivered hot and fresh the moment the locks on our cells were clicked open.

Our block was out, and everyone was on the move to get to breakfast and figure out what the fuck was going on. I walked past the cell to see if I could make out what happened, but the yellow tape made it nearly impossible to get a good look inside. We were all curious, but we all knew better than to ask openly about somebody's business, especially in open settings when the guards were on high alert.

"Yeah, man, that young bul ain't have no business being in that cell with that man," I overheard one of the old heads saying. I kneeled over to act like I was tying my boots up just so I could listen in for as long as I could. "They said Cold Blooded was right there when it happened. He could've stopped it, but he didn't. Not fast enough, at least."

My stomach turned, just thinking about what could have happened inside that cell. I was closing in on my fifth year, and that was the first time I had seen caution tape sprawled across a cell like that. I looked up from my boot strings when the old heads got quiet. They were onto my fifty-two-fakeout and cut their conversation short.

"Nah, pardon me, OG, it ain't like that. These fucking boot strings keep coming loose," I said, trying to play it off. One thing about me is I always gave respect to the old heads. The OGs are the heartbeat of the system. They were going to know and hear things before a lot of us younger cats did, so I knew keeping them in close proximity was one of the smartest things I could do.

The chow hall had a different energy to it. There was a very distinct divide between racial groups, even more so than usual. The cafeteria was typically separated between races, gangs, and neighborhoods, but today, the white boys were a lot tighter knit in how they eyeballed the brothers and even the Puerto Ricans. It was safe to assume that whatever happened, a white boy was involved, and nine times out of ten, he was the victim.

I grabbed my tray and got in line for my morning slop. Once the line started to move, I noticed Ray was in the chow line a few guys behind me. I motioned to about five of them to let them go ahead of me so that I could low-key ask Ray what had happened. Letting people cut you in line wasn't always the greatest idea, especially while there was a silent war brewing, because you never knew, you might end up just two people short of the last scoop of Cream of Wheat, and you'd be dead and stink'n, starved until the next meal if your commissary stash isn't up.

Ray was the only person I would trust to ask at that moment because he was level-headed and went out of his way to stay low profile and off the radar. You just never knew sometimes. A motherfucker would randomly get loud and cause a scene just 'cause they woke up on the wrong side of their paper-thin mattress. *"Man, what the fuck are you asking me for? I ain't in them people's business, young bul!"* That was the type of shit anyone on weirdo time might bust out with at the top of their lungs just to stir up and cause some drama. Boredom and isolation will do that to you. You'd find entertainment in the most ignorant of ways, depending on the mood. But I knew Ray would never step out of line like that. He had too much to lose. Besides, Ray and I started to form a bond when he helped me study for the GED and answered many of my questions about business and entrepreneurship. Ray was smart as fuck, but he definitely wasn't nobody's chump.

"Aye, Ray, what's the word? What's with the yellow tape and shit?" I asked, my hand rubbing my mouth so no one could read my lips and figure out what we were talking about.

"Not here, Slim. I'll get with you in the law library when we're done." I could tell by his tone that whatever took place, he didn't want any part of it—not even as the messenger.

We walked to our table with trays filled with food we really had no interest in eating, but it's prison life, and you got to do what you got to do. If you don't eat the food provided to you and you lose too much weight, you could easily become somebody else's food as a lightweight. Three hots and a cot and whatever else you could come up with was the difference between getting rag-dolled or molly-whopped if your hand game wasn't up. We sat down and made up some bullshit small talk here and there just to cut through the tension that was growing in the air. Without saying much, we both stood up almost at the exact same time, collected our trays, and started to make our way to the law library to discuss what the big mystery was.

As usual, the law library was so empty you could hear an ant pissing on cotton. I had gotten used to the stillness of the space over the last few months. This was where I came to focus on my exam and learn some things outside of the normal everyday board games and prison gossip. Ray was a huge help in getting my math and reading levels up to par to pass the practice exams with flying colors, but what I enjoyed the most was all the knowledge he had about marketing and finance. I could honestly say he was one of the inspirations for me to turn over a new leaf even behind bars. He put me on to a game I had never even thought of, and it opened my mind up to some major opportunities that were available to me when I finally got my high school equivalency diploma and got out of there.

"So, remember the kid who came through here a few weeks ago— the Irish kid who claimed he was half Puerto Rican?" Ray asked, holding in a laugh at the half-PR stunt the ginger redhead tried to pull off.

"Yeah, I do. What about him?"

"Well, he ended up . . ." and before Ray finished telling me, Mitch and his crew walked in, causing Ray to pause midsentence. Ray said, "Bet we'll catch up later. Good luck on the test," and gave me a pound on his way out. I was mad as a motherfucker. I wanted the details of what went down without all the extra jailbird twists and turns. Those dudes liked to hype stories up and put the ten on the two. They would add bullshit to the fifth power even when the truth was already wild enough.

Mitch and the crew sat down with books they checked out as if they were about to read or attempt to be productive. That was the best way to keep guards from swarming around, trying to ear hustle on the shit only the inmates knew.

"Aye, you ain't gonna believe this shit," Smurf said, laughing and smiling ear to ear.

"Chill, Smurf," Mitch said while gesturing to lower his volume and calm it down with his hands.

"Okay, okay, bet . . . you know the little redhead cracka, right?" Smurf whispered. "Well, yeah, his ass got raped last night."

My heart dropped into my stomach as I looked around at the three others at the table. Everyone had the same look of disgust.

"Whoa, whoa, whoa. Hold up, man! What? Who did it?" I said, trying to keep my voice down and flipping through the pages of my book, pretending like I was reading.

"You know that wasn't nobody but Beast. They said he fucked that boy so hard up the ass that the bag of quan burst, and that's what killed him."

"Wait, what do you mean? He's dead?" I said, trying to wrap my head around what Smurf was saying.

"Yeah, what do you think the yellow tape was for? That boy got straight fucked to death!" The guys at the table let out an uncomfortable laugh.

"Damn, Smurf, you just say any old fucking thing. Chill," Mitch said, shaking his head at Smurf.

"But wait, what's quan? You lost me with that one," I asked.

"You know, those the pills these burnouts go crazy for."

Quan, I learned, was short for Sinequan, one of a few antidepressants inmates can get to help survive their sentence without losing their minds. Some actually needed it, but most just wanted another way to get high. (Chi-chi's was a staple meal between chow times made up of ramen noodles and whatever else you had to throw in a pot. But chi-chi-quans was a mixture of Oodles of Noodles, tuna if you had some, nachos, and Sinequan.)

Smurf continued: "Irish Red was supposed to be moving them between the blocks 'cause nobody would suspect him, but he got shaken up and swallowed the whole stash when Cold Blooded came around shaking shit up. Beast must have said fuck it, let me get a two-for-one 'cause he fucked that boy around something serious, hoping that the bag of quan would fall out in his shit or something. But that never happened. The word is he left him curled up on the floor, and the bag must've ripped open in his stomach or something. They said when it finally released, it came shooting out his ass hard as hell like a pressure washer foaming with bloody diarrhea. It must've been a lot of backed-up air in his shitter from all that pounding. There was shit and blood everywhere. It was so bad that Beast called for the C.O.s his damn self."

The silence at the table was deafening. None of us could ever imagine that happening to one of us, but what if it did? There were other men there just like Beast that were just as huge: six-six, 260-pound booty bandits walking around just waiting for an unsuspecting victim. If they wanted to take you down, there wasn't shit you could really do if you didn't have a sword strapped on you.

"Now, this is where you come in, Slim," Mitch said, looking grimly at me.

"Huh, what do you mean? I ain't got shit to do with this," I shot back.

"I'm not saying you did; I'm saying here's where we need you."

My face scrunched up as I looked around to see the crew with all eyes on me too.

"You've been cool this whole time; you kept your name clean. You don't have any write-ups and no time in the hole. Your name is almost as good as gold when it comes to the C.O.s. We need you to do the runs now. The Sinequan that Red was moving for us was coming straight from the psych ward, with Mrs. Walker being the only warden to have keys to get in and out whenever she wanted. That bitch likes you, Lo. And you got Ray in your pocket now too. This should be easy for you as long as you don't swallow the work like dumbass ginger red just did."

They all laughed quietly but still with an intensity that stated, *"We're not asking you; we're telling you."*

I was done. My chest felt like I had a collapsed lung. *Nah, this can't be happening. God, please. Help me!*

DEAR FREEDOM,

I know it's been a minute since I've written you, but I've been staying busy, not wanting to complain to you. Who would've known that the closer I got to independence, the more challenging standing alone would become? I've always been a follower; you know that. The consequences of my poor decisions and being a follower snatched me from you, leading me to years of inhumane confinement, years stolen from my short time on this planet—years that no one but myself stole simply because I couldn't stand up on my thoughts and morals and just be okay with being myself. I was afraid; I think I still am.

Something different is happening inside me. Something that is yearning for a change. I can only imagine this feeling is similar to what a dope fiend feels when their high is coming down. I want to run, but there's nowhere to run to. I want to scream, but there are consequences for that too.

Freedom, you are breaking me in places I didn't even know existed. The thought of you and your absence is so painful that I sometimes feel like I could hurt myself just to prove how much to you.

And yet, you're still my greatest motivation. I miss you. I need you . . .

I'm gone.

Wallo

I WOULD BE A LIAR if I told you I wasn't strategically involved in the criminal enterprise while behind bars. No one gets off that easy to where you don't have to earn your stay, whether you like it or not. There's always some trade-off for your life when living in prison. Some will have it way worse than others, depending on the energy you put out there, like what happened to Red. He walked around with his chest poked out like he was tough and ended up dead in a six-by-six prison cell with his ass blown out. Don't get me wrong, I'm not saying what happened to Red was his fault, but I am saying that certain energy attracts certain responses, and in that environment, playing certain roles was similar to rolling dice with your life. I never did the tough-guy act. I knew exactly what that would get me. Play that role, and you will be checked and tested regularly until you either catch a body or someone snatches yours.

Until now, my interaction within the crime circles had gone undetected. I hadn't had a single incident where I was caught or ratted on for my involvement in any activities that could have extended my sentence. I played a mean game of cat and mouse with the law, and I'd like to think that I didn't get caught because I was clever, but I'm sure it had less to do with that and more to do with God having a bigger plan in store. You know how they say, "God protects fools and babies." It wasn't always easy figuring out ways to contribute to the community of cellies that held me down, but I definitely chose to serve in ways that took less risk and offered more rewards, that's for sure.

One of the most rewarding stunts I would pull was pretending to be the middleman between a commissary bully and a rookie inmate who didn't have the proper support system to get him through his days untouched.

"Aye, man, I don't know what you did to get green-lit, but once you got that target on your back, you're about to have a real fucked-up time in here unless you comply," I would say to a newly processed inmate, a first-timer, or someone transferred from another prison who was getting punked before reaching our cellblock. The game was negotiating commissary money and contraband brought in by one of the rookie's family members or friends to keep the bullies off his ass while generating some cash for our cells. Believe it or not, in some twisted way, although it was still fucked up, I felt this scheme was a noble position as it kept the rookies from getting tossed up. On one side, it gave the newjack a sense of safety by having someone who could go between him and a crazed man shaking him down. Still, on the other side, I was playing a part in extorting someone's family, who would do just about anything to keep them alive or un-hurt, including risk their own freedom by smuggling contraband in during visits.

The upside was the risks in these transactions were minimal for me. I came off as the peacemaker, the hero in a sense. However, the downside was the moral weight it carried, knowing someone's preg-nant wife used their infant daughter's diaper to transport drugs to cover the cost of being protected by me and from goons who would otherwise take his life.

Like golf, it was a constant game of opposites. Looking at it, it felt like I was killing three birds with one stone—and no one got hurt unless someone got caught. This was exactly one of those examples of what "being armed with good intentions" meant to me at the time. The con game gave me the advantage of being personable in situations where others would have felt the need to strong-arm.

Hear me out: If anyone ever thought prison was meant to reform, they're sadly mistaken. If your entire foundation has been built on criminal intentions, what other skill would you have to lean on when your day-to-day survival depends on negotiations? It's partly the reason why it's such a revolving door. You come in and accidentally figure out how to become an even sharper criminal.

Over the past few months, I spent much of my time reading and researching ideas for things I could do once I got out. I became obsessed with marketing and its similarity to the con game, only it was legal. Between running extortion schemes and being the intermediary for transactions, I started implementing some of the skills I learned from master marketing books on some prison officials. I figured that if I could learn how to market new ideas and change their perspective, I could, without a doubt, market myself to the parole board in ways that would help them buy the bullshit I was selling.

Let's be real here: The board don't want to hear anyone's sob stories of why they felt they weren't good enough or how their daddy left them and made them feel like less than a man once they became adults. No. They want you to wear whatever crime you were locked up for on your chest, whether you were truly guilty or not. They are out for blood and want you to repent with every breath. They want you to prove you are a changed person and that what you did to serve time was the most significant mistake you've ever committed. They want you to beg without sounding like you're begging—you know, because God forbid you're actually willing to grovel for your freedom. If you did, you'd be deemed unsuitable and might even end up on psych meds.

I knew I had to strategize and lube every word I said in my parole meeting to at least learn what it took to appease those parole board assholes. So, I stayed up late and read till my eyes were bloodshot. I was emotionally prepared to be denied parole because I knew better than to get my hopes up on my first hoe stroll before the board. Still, I was also prepared to shake the tree of knowledge and see exactly what words and body language gave me an advantage. It was a losing game at this stage, but gaining the know-how was worth the countless hours of preparedness.

BETWEEN THE TIMES I SPENT engaged in my new obsession of reading and researching, I would drift off in my bunk, sometimes just daydreaming, and Brenda would come to me almost like a ghost of times lost. Getting lost in the sauce is what we'd call it. Dreaming with your eyes wide open. Not quite sleeping, but not fully conscious.

Brenda wasn't the only girl I had that got me wide open, but the real deal is that she was the first and the worst of any girl, to be honest. To keep it a buck, I'm not sure she was even my girl. I have to laugh at how gone I was off that lady when I think about it. Before I was locked up, Brenda had a full-grown man doing time in the pen, and when he would call, I would keep quiet whenever she had to accept a collect call from him. I guess I was the side jawn to her real nigga, who she was holding down until his time was up. I couldn't give less of a fuck because I was reaping all the perks and rewards in his absence. As soon as she hung up with the goofball, we would get right back to work like he never even existed.

"Lo baby, hand me that jar of honey; let me show you something," Brenda said with a kitten's purr. That was her normal tone that went unnoticed after a while of getting to know her. She was always so smooth in her delivery of everything, whether it was dope deals, pick-ups and drop-offs, or some freaky sexy shit she would be kicking on the phone with her boo in the clink. Her voice was like a silky, sensual hum from a ghetto snake charmer.

We would spend hours at her condo downtown just kicking it. She would put me on to all the new luxury pieces that came out that season, be it clothes, shoes, furniture, or whatever lit her eyes up. When she saw something she really loved in a magazine, Brenda would lick the tip of her finger, slide it down the ear of each page, and fold it at the corner so she could remember where her next high-end purchases would come from. The shit was slick and would turn me on.

"Keep up the good work, baby. You'll have a place just like this too someday," she'd say.

"I don't need none of this fancy shit; I like it just the way it is. You keep letting me work, I'm gonna get my paper up and get my Nanny a new house, and my mom, too. I'm supercool on all that, I promise you," I would say just to hide my embarrassment. I wanted more for myself, of course, but I just knew the route I was going wouldn't be long-lived. I hated never being able to fully step into the role of a big-time dope dealer. Something about it made me feel small, and knowing that I could never fill my father's shoes in the dope game was one of the main reasons.

I returned from the kitchen with the jar of honey she'd asked me for. I was so impressed by how she transferred all her condiments and seasonings to fancier containers so you wouldn't see all the tacky supermarket labels. I applied the little details I picked up just by being around her to other areas of my life. I learned that baggies in specific

< A mom's love:
  my mother
  and me in the
  early '80s.

>
All of Jackie's boys
together: my older
brother, Steven;
me; and our
younger brother,
Jalil, in 1986.

< With my
  stepfather
  Hip, Jalil,
  and Steven,
  ca. 1987.

< Showing off my savings, ca. 1991

∧ With my friend Little Larry in the early '90s.

< Jalil and Jackie visiting at SCI Dallas in 1998.

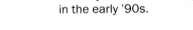

>
At Vision Quest in 1994 with friends I made in the program. I am on the far right.

Graduating
with my GED
at SCI Dallas
in 1999.

Back home:
on 13th Street
in Philadelphia
in 2001 after
returning from
SCI Dallas.

Cousin Gillie visiting me at
Gratersford Prison in 2008.

Steven and my prison IDs
from our time in SCI Dallas.

INMATE
DG2670

WALLACE

PEEPLES

PA Department of Corrections

INMATE
FF6732

STEVEN

PEEPLES

^
My nephew
Mukson, about
seven years
old, paying
me a visit at
Gratersford
Prison.

>
Me and
Jackie at
Gratersford
Prison, 2013.

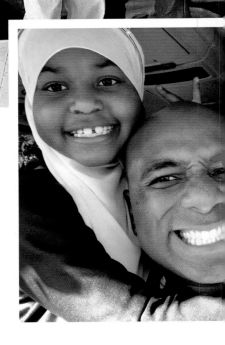

<
Steven
and his
daughter
MayMay
together,
ca. late
2011.

>
With my
niece,
MayMay,
when she
was eight
years old
in 2017.

< Flowers for
  Nanny, 2018.

> Gillie's wife, Regina; his daughter
  Nyla, also known as N3WYRKLA;
  Gillie; and me at the Roots
  Picnic 2024 in Philadelphia after
  Nyla's musical performance.

< With Gillie at our podcast
  producer Kevin Kilkenny's
  wedding, 2023.

^ I took Nanny to the Philadelphia
  Auto Show, 2022.

∨
Beating the
students at
Morehouse
College in
Connect 4 after
being invited
to speak at the
college, March
2023.

>
With my
favorite
singer,
Sampha,
in 2023.

∧
MayMay
and me at
her middle
school
graduation
in 2024.

>
My good
friend Sife
and me.
We met in
1998 in SCI
Dallas and
have been
friends
ever since.

With my ride-or-die friend Shay Lawson and record producer Jermaine Dupri during YouTube Avenues Atlanta, 2023.

I was called by the NFL to speak to the Rookies: first up were the Giants in May 2023.

Behind the scenes at my television debut on Issa Rae's *Rap Sh!t*, April 2023.

With my manager Des on our way to our *Rap Sh!t* shooting, equally excited and nervous.

My daughter Day Day and me on the day of her college graduation from Lincoln University in May 2024.

> Signing my first book deal for *Armed with Good Intentions*, March 31, 2023.

With Mike Scott, the executive director of Philadelphia Juvenile Justice Services Center, after I received an award from the Philadelphia Youth Study Center, November 2023.

colors and packaging were eye-catching and seemed to bring the dope fiends back to my mother's sunroom for the re-up faster than others.

One thing was for sure: Brenda always took it easy on me. She knew I wasn't cut out to be a kingpin, nor did she want that from me. I was like a little puppy with my tail wagging, just happy to be around, pick up some game, and stack a little money. She had other ideas for me.

When I came back to her room, Brenda had nothing but an emerald-green lace bra and panties on. Green is my favorite color. I wondered if she knew or even gave a fuck, honestly. This was the moment I was patiently waiting for. Before now, we hadn't really done anything more than a couple rub and tugs here and there. I didn't think she would ever take me seriously enough to actually go all the way.

"Come over here and lay down." She patted her queen-size pink satin sheets. I walked over and sat on the edge of the bed, thinking I was definitely in over my head.

"Nuh-uh, take them funky street clothes off! We don't do that over here," she yelled.

I stripped down faster than Clark Kent could turn into Superman. She pulled me back by my shoulders and told me to lay still. *Ah shit,* I thought. *It's about to get real.* Let me tell you, it doesn't matter how much of a horndog you may be in these settings; there's a weird vulnerability that comes with being told what to do while lying in a position of submission with a woman ten times more experienced than you.

I remember clearly laying back and closing my eyes tight, and the next thing I knew, honey was poured all over me from top to bottom. Brenda was kissing and sucking trails of honey off every inch of my body. When she got to my whip, the warmth from her mouth and the stickiness from her honey-coated lips made my eyes pop open. I had to see with my two good eyes just what kind of magic she was working on me. *I can't believe this shit! I think I might love this bitch!*

The noise from inmates coming in from the yard snapped me back to reality. I closed my eyes again and hung on to the vision of Brenda and me for as long as possible. Maybe it was too long because I saw a mental glimpse of my then thirteen-year-old aroused naked body in that instant.

"I was just a kid," my inner voice echoed as I was hit with gut-wrenching nausea. Inmates started walking along the tier loudly and disorderly, distracting me from a revelation I desperately needed to process. Brenda was just shy of thirty at the time.

"Was she a pedophile?" I whispered as I shook my head. "How could this feel so wrong now when at the time it felt so right?" I mean, I guess it didn't feel right then, either. I was just okay with feeling like I was a man and like I was getting away with something. But I wasn't. She was. "My innocence," I gasped.

"WHAT'S THE WORD, YOUNG BUL?" A familiar voice broke through my puzzled thoughts. It was Ray's voice coming from the entryway to my cell. His tone was cheerful, but his facial expression quickly changed. His face went from his typical cool-cat demeanor to concern as I sat up and he saw the grim look on my face. "Aye, man, you good? You look like you just saw a ghost," he said while looking over his shoulders for oncoming inmate foot traffic. There's only so much concern one inmate can show for another before rumors of funny business start flying without much effort.

"Shit, damn near," I replied, swallowing hard to repress the urge to hurl my ramen across the cell.

"Shake that shit off," Ray said, without even asking what was wrong. "Leave what's outside outside! You heard? You can only deal with what's right in front of you, one day at a time. Besides"—he paused while shaking an envelope in his hand—"you got good news coming to you straight from the messenger man."

I jumped up and nearly snatched the envelope out of his hand.

"Good job, my boy," he said as I stood there in shock that I had passed my GED exam!

"Oh shit. We did this shit, man!" I yelled.

"Nah, you did that. You kept your head down and got to those books like I told you, and you figured it out for yourself," Ray said.

I couldn't help but feel the tug of emotions and confusion lingering over me. On the one hand, I couldn't believe this news. But on the other, I had just realized that I had been sexually assaulted as a child; it was something I had never even considered. I shook my head and tried to stay in the moment. But I could see by the look on Ray's face that he, too, could tell I was feeling conflicted.

"Anyway, congrats, young'n," he said, extending his hand for a pound before walking back to his cell.

Prison isn't really the place to seek clarity on topics, specifically topics concerning sexuality, so I wasn't about to invite Ray into my inner feelings like that. Most men tell these stories with their chests poked out as a badge of honor. I once did too, when I didn't think anything was wrong with the sick shit that was going on.

I would pop my shit, telling all the guys back in the juvenile detention building how I was fucking and slinging packs for a kingpin's old lady. Even though I'm positive more than half of them thought I was bullshitting, I told those stories with pride, like I was really out there doing something worth stripes.

Just thinking about it, my palms became clammy. In one hand, I held the results of my hard work and dedication. *Wow, I got a passing score on my GED*, I thought, beaming. And with the other I palmed my face, trying to rub away the compilation of tarnished memories of being a victim of a woman who took sexual advantage of me.

I decided I wouldn't let the dark clouds hang over my head and dampen the excitement of my fantastic feedback. So, I shook it off and thought it would be a great time to call home and give Jackie the amazing news.

As I walked out of my cell, envelope still in hand, I questioned many parts of my life that I now needed to understand. I paused every few steps, wondering where my mother was when certain things happened. I pondered whether I had the right to ask anything at all of her when I was the one making the terrible decisions. With every step, there was a different emotion. I felt victimized and abandoned with the right step, and with the left, I felt like I was definitely stone-cold trip'n. *Dog, you got some ass and sold some drugs off your momma's porch. What the fuck is so wrong with that?* I asked myself so many questions that by the time I reached the phone, I realized the call to my mother shouldn't happen.

HIT DOGS HOLLER

A FEW BIG HATS CAME STORMING through the building one day, ripping through every cell on every tier, searching for smut mags and contraband like rabid dogs. Stormtroopers flipped our beds, knocked over shelves that held our family pics, and ransacked every bit of whatever personal items we had left to our names like none of it was worth shit. Hundreds of inmates yelled out "Fuck the police" and whatever other wild shit they could think of, but that was about all they could do. The big hats are almost never met with too much resistance. Their power is swifter than that of the day-to-day C.O.s, and you can find yourself in the hole for at least a year in the blink of an eye for just looking crazy if you're not careful. The big hats are not the ones you want to fuck with. Ever!

Big hats are what we called the warden and his team of higher-ranking officers. The supreme dickheads, not the little ones who wore the goofy, bootleg cardboard-looking caps we dealt with regularly. Every so often, these motherfuckers would find something new to fuck with us over. For whatever reason, this time around, smut magazines and anything that showed a fat ass and some titties were the targets. There's something sick and twisted about wanting to punish a man further while he's already being punished. Today was the day a new rule was being passed, and any type of adult content found on the premises would be considered contraband, and you would receive a hit for it. A hit is another form of punishment on top of punishment, another prison inside of a prison, the hole just for minding your fucking business.

The announcement of the new rule came from left field and sent shockwaves through the cellblocks, one level after another. Two thousand men were locked away in those cages without the look, smell, or touch of a woman for years, some for life, and their idea was to rid us of the last remnants we had of them. This shit had to fall under cruel and unusual punishment. The yelling from heated inmates echoed through the tiers, causing ripples of uneasy glances and whispers of late-night riots once the big hats left.

We got lucky, though, Mitch and I; our cell was already cleared of everything else before they got there, except for a few black-tail magazines that starred my favorite freak hoe ever, Pinky. Goddamn, I loved that hoe something special. But gratefully, there were no drugs or shanks or anything out of the ordinary in our cell that would have made my life hell.

After Red was killed, we were all put on an intense lockdown. We were subjected to a strict twenty-three-and-one for weeks. There was no yard, no visitations, and sometimes days would pass before being let out for showers. There were always going to be fights, stabbings, and rapes while in prison; that was a given. But when the warden got word that Red's body cavity was stuffed with over a hundred different pills, they had to shut everything down, including medical treatment. They came to the conclusion that there was no way that many drugs were coming in just from the streets, so it forced them to start running internal investigations on everyone from the officers to the nurses and everyone else on down before the media got wind of it.

The cell raids couldn't have happened at a better time. Lockdown saved me from having to step up and become the transporter of all the drugs and shit Red wasn't around to do anymore. Not having to worry about getting caught up in some major work that I wanted no part of bought me time to start thinking of ways to make my time here easier if I wasn't getting out anytime soon.

For the past eighteen months, I'd gone through every program the state offered to position myself for an early release. I made it my business to get on the list as soon as I became eligible to apply for the programs, which is twenty-three months before my minimum sentence. I asked around and spoke with my old heads about the process and what they thought I could do to make myself a better candidate, but they didn't seem as interested or confident in the program as I was then. Most of them laughed and called me a newjack, and none of them hesitated to remind me that I was a habitual offender and the cards were stacked against me.

I couldn't get with their mentality. I figured we had nothing to lose, so why not try our hand anyway? One thing I knew for a fact was the time would go by anyway, so I might as well shoot my shot and, at the very least, learn something new in the process.

☐ ☐ ☐

SLEEP WASN'T GOING TO COME easy that night. I was just twenty-four hours away from finding out the state's decision, which takes a few months after I attended my parole hearing, on whether I was approved to blow this joint. I was restless, tossing and turning so much that my neck hurt. Mentally exhausted, I lay on my back, tracing the cracks in the ceiling, imagining every winding one was a roadway back to Nanny's place.

Jogging down memory lane didn't serve me much because it made me wonder what I was in such a rush to get back out for. Of course, it was the luxury of freedom, money, cars, and hoes from the second I touched the turf, but I hadn't devised a real plan, something I could get into that would keep me from ending up in another jam. I knew for sure I was going to drop a mixtape. I had too much shit to say not to put it over a beat, but right now, I had less than twenty-four hours before I visited with the early release counselor, and I know for damn sure rapping wouldn't be a convincing enough job description for her to sign the approval form. I had eighteen months to figure that shit out, and all I'd thought of was this: I'm going to drop a mixtape, design clothes, and do a whole bunch of other shit niggas from my hood have never done. *Was this another setup for failure?* I had to ask myself.

Everyone, including me, knew that getting your heart set on an early release on a first attempt was a suicide mission. Yet, I still allowed the idea of going home to pierce my heart with killer precision. As much as it may have seemed like I had become well-adjusted to prison life, I wasn't—it was all a facade. I had created ulcers in my stomach from wrestling with the thought of having to pay for my mistakes with my life, and I wanted out.

Please let me out. Please let me out. Please let me out.

I squeezed my eyes shut, trying to block out the pleading voice in my head, begging God or anyone who would listen to free me from this hell. Panic attacks—before I knew what those were—had a strange way of creeping up on me when I least expected them. The panic was so intense I felt myself losing the fight to its redundant pattern of begging over and over again. I grabbed my head with both hands and felt my grip nearly crushing my skull. The panic inside me was so loud I couldn't think clearly over my raging thoughts. It was like my internal hysteria was being projected over a loudspeaker. I was almost sure everyone could hear me. My breathing became shallow, my palms sweaty, and my throat felt like it was closing. Time was ticking, and I was growing more and more nervous with every second. I don't remember a time when I had to battle the voice in my head this hard or it ever being this loud.

Just when I felt like I could be having a real-life heart attack, *BOOM BOOM*. Two banging noises came from beneath my bunk and scared the living shit out of me. Mitch kicked the fuck out of my bunk twice and angrily said, "Cut that shit out, man. You already know what's going to happen."

I sat in a cold sweat, trying to take in his words. He was right, and I suddenly became fueled with anger, too, knowing I had just allowed myself to become drunk with foolish delusion.

Boy, you're fucking losing it, I thought to myself. Still, at that moment, I was aware I was tripping, and it triggered a split personality—a loosening grip on myself and reality. It was the audacity of hope that fucked my head up, and the only way to prevent it from seeping too deep into my skull was to laugh at how stupid I was for allowing hope to put me in a chokehold.

I might've gotten all of two, maybe three hours of sleep that night, but when it was time for the morning count, I was full of energy as if I was geeked up on something. I couldn't help but notice the look on Mitch's face that morning. It was like he was disgusted by my anxiousness or something worse. I wondered if he had started hating on me quietly. What if he thought I did have a chance at early release, and he hated that it was me and not him? I grabbed my head with both hands again, shaking off the intrusive thoughts, realizing that this new head-grabbing, head-shaking, and uninvited voice in my head was starting to become something I had to overcome. *Man, I'm really fucking tripping. Get it together!*

I couldn't help but think about the time and dedication I put in to get to this moment. According to what was in my files, I should have been considered a success as far as it went for the programs I'd attended. I maintained a clean record and a decent job in the kitchen, even if it was just cutting up thousands upon thousands of potatoes. I felt I deserved to go home.

From what I heard, whether it be an early release program or parole, it is just a numbers game, and no one truly gives a fuck about whether or not you were honorable while doing your time. In an early release program, instead of serving your full sentence, you're released from prison to a halfway house. If they needed to clear out fifty beds for a fresh batch of new prisoners, fifty heads would be set free at random. I've heard of guys with clean records who have completed several programs getting denied, and cats that have fucked up in major ways get approved. It was simply the luck of the draw. But nine out of ten times, your first go-round is as good as denied, perfect gentleman or not.

One thing I knew for sure was that I wasn't about to eat a damn thing from the chow hall. It would be my luck to fuck around and shit myself on the way to see the council. My nerves got so jacked up that it felt like my stomach was about to drop from under me. I've seen that happen to other buls before; stomachs got so fucked up before meeting the board that they shit the floor.

Besides, I didn't want anyone or anything to throw me off my game. I was on high alert, so I decided to fall back from chow and everything until it was time for my visit to hear the verdict. While I waited, I thought a lot about my brother Steven and how the lives we were both living might kill us before we had an opportunity to change.

I sat on the cold, paint-chipped stool fixed to the cell's thin metal desk, waiting for the time to pass. I thought about writing a letter to Freedom, but I became too overwhelmed with visions of Steve's body sprawled across Nanny's basement floor with holes in him. I looked around my cell, hoping something would catch my attention so I wouldn't travel down this road of memories again. *Not now.*

I remember lying through my teeth when telling intake counselors at the juvenile detention centers that I would snort up a fifty-piece of coke once a week for recreation. That was a lie from the pit of hell. I didn't have the balls to do it, no matter how fun some of Steven's older friends made it seem. There were times when I was tempted just to prove I was as cool as they were. But I was always too observant, and I saw firsthand what it did to my people. I watched how it changed them almost overnight—specifically, how quickly it changed the people around me that I looked up to.

So why did I lie to those juvie counselors? Because being classified as a drug user or addict came with some privileges inside the institutions, from special activities and programs to extra time with counselors shooting the shit about a whole lot of nothing. Anything was better than sitting in your dorm, bored to tears. I figured I'd just lie and cash in on what little fake sympathy they had left—sympathy that was typically only granted to junior dust heads and crack babies.

Everything I did and said was some act of survival. I lived by the famous Law 21 from *48 Laws of Power*: "Play a sucker to catch a sucker." I never had an issue with playing dumber than my mark. So, a cokehead I was as long as it came with some type of reward.

My trip back in time came to a crashing end when I heard my name being barked by an officer over the PA system. It was still early, and I didn't expect to be called to the counselor's office until later in the afternoon. Now, all of a sudden, I started feeling sick again, like I was about to throw up last night's ramen. If I didn't know any better, I would think my ankles were shackled to the desk. The way I moved felt so slow; it was like walking through quicksand.

"Alright, fuck it," I said. "Let's just get the shit over with so I can get back to doing my time without the mental nagging of the begging-ass voices in my head." But there was another part of me that questioned how I would take the news if I were granted my freedom. I pictured myself screaming like a prostitute who had just won a scratch-off lottery ticket. The thought of that made me laugh so hard that I caught a few glances from people looking at me like I'd lost my damn mind.

"Have a seat, Peeples."

I walked in, sat at the wooden desk, mean mugging, and waited for my denial slip, almost as if I wanted it. That's just how badly I wanted to protect myself from the blowback of hearing that it wasn't a favorable decision.

"The State of Pennsylvania has found you suitable for early release, Inmate Peeples. Your pending release will be set within thirty days of this meeting. You will be required to spend the next year in an appointed halfway house, where you will be required to have gainful employment until your determined length of stay has expired and not a day less. Do you understand, Mr. Peeples?"

I was frozen. I couldn't think, hear, talk, or move.

"Is that understood, Peeples?"

"Hell yeah, I understood! I mean, yes, ma'am."

I couldn't believe I was one of the lucky random motherfuckers to be granted early release on my first attempt. I wanted to scream, fall to my knees, and pray. I was flooded with so much emotion that I had to be reminded that good news doesn't always travel best behind these walls, and some things are better left unsaid.

We went over the requirements for my release and the commitments I had to meet in order to fulfill my obligations to the state. The counselor might as well have been speaking another language because I had lost all comprehension by that point and couldn't care less about anything else she had to say. In my head, I could already feel the sun on my face and a crisp, cool breeze. I knew the first person I had to call would be my cousin Gillie. He would make sure I had a fresh outfit ready for the day of my release.

I signed my paperwork without reading a single word. The counselor let out a slight laugh and wished me luck.

"Thank you, Ms. Umm, Ms. Umm . . . Counselor!"

"I hope never to see you again, Mr. Peeples!"

Words could not explain how happy I was, but as quickly as that feeling came over me, it just as quickly got lost. From the moment I stepped out of the office, it felt like all eyes were on me—eyes that didn't appear to be the friendliest. What I wasn't prepared for was the feeling that I'd be walking through a field of land mines while walking back to my cell.

I was positive no one overheard the news given to me, but it was as if there was a line of hungry wolves waiting for any reason to let loose, and I was the food.

I had at least thirty days to stay out of the way.

The old heads warned me a while back that cats would try to trick me out of my freedom. They'd start some shit with me just to give the state a reason to renege on my release and keep my ass locked up in here with them. There was no way I was about to let that happen, so I kept my head down and put on a mean poker face as I walked through the halls. I even bypassed the phones so that it looked like I had no good reason to call home.

Chow was just coming to an end, and everyone was on the move to their next destination. There was a small group of inmates being escorted through the central area chain-gang style, which meant it must've been a prison-to-prison transfer.

Once I got past them, I paused immediately from a delayed reaction. *I know that can't be him*, I thought to myself, but when I turned back around, what I thought I saw was confirmed: Baby D was standing there chained ankle to ankle, staring right back at me.

"Oh shit, how you be?" I said. I'm hoping he missed my shocked facial expression.

We both nodded as to say what's up, but there was a tension between us that even the C.O. picked up.

"Turn the fuck around, newbie," the officer shouted at Baby D. As he turned his head back toward the direction they were moving, I took off running without warning, the same way I did the last time I saw him.

The streets were quiet, and no one had heard from Baby D in years. Rumor was that he was either dead, hog-tied in someone's basement, or on the run in another state. I never cared too much to ask or investigate. As far as I was concerned, wherever he was still wasn't far enough away. But now here he was. Maybe he was extradited here from whatever state he went into hiding. Either way, I wanted no part of him, and although I still, to this day, cannot fully understand what really happened that night, what I do know is that I don't want to find out.

All I had was thirty days to stay the fuck out of the way from anything or anyone that could knock me off my square.

I had thirty days to devise a plan to blow up my mixtape and hit the road with Cousin Gill.

I couldn't believe I had only thirty days to get my mind right and get the fuck up out of here.

Those thirty days started to feel closer to a year.

BY THE TIME I WAS ready to tell the truth about my release date, word had already started buzzing that I was on my way out. I tried to convince a few people that my paperwork was being held up by one of the higher-ups and that I wasn't sure if I'd been approved, but most of them had heard this same bullshit from other people and knew I was bluffing. The good thing is I didn't make any mortal enemies during my time there. I clowned and tap danced my way out of plenty of awkward situations that could have cost me my life, and I could honestly say God had to have been on my side for me to have avoided so many positions that others have not survived.

I had two weeks left on my sentence before I would be free when I received a note that Baby D wanted to speak to me.

What's up, young bul? Long time no see. Word is you're about to flee the coop, and I might not get the chance to chop it up with you. They got me in the hole for a buck and a quarter, so I hope this message makes its way to you. Look, do me a favor. Don't come back here, Slim. Don't make the same mistakes. I never want to see your face again in this place.

IT WOULD BE A BALD-FACED lie to say I wasn't exactly sure how to take the note. The tone of Baby D's words wasn't specific enough for me to think everything was as good as gold, especially how things left off years ago. A dose of paranoia set in, and the thought that his words could have been an undercover threat made me nauseous. I couldn't have been a happier nigga at that moment because I would be long gone before they brought Baby D back to the general population.

Back in the library, there was a guy named Rick, whom I got to know the past few months while I busied myself with reading self-help and motivational books and whatever else I could get my hands on to keep me occupied and out of trouble. Rick was an older cat, somewhere in his late fifties; he had a maple-brown complexion and a well-kept, tapered beard. I was too embarrassed to tell him he reminded me of my father. I had a hard time trying to process that feeling for myself. I imagined if my father were alive at his age, he would have a similar demeanor. Rick was smooth but wasn't very talkative; he seemed to always have something he was trying to figure out, the same way I pictured my father to be—a cool, laid-back mastermind.

One day, I accidentally picked up one of the books he placed on the table next to my pile before checking it out. It was a book titled *The Spook Who Sat by the Door*. When I noticed it wasn't mine, I put it back down and whispered, "My bad."

Rick replied, "Nah, that one is for you. Give it a try and see what you think."

I flipped the book from front to back, pretending to be interested in what was on the cover, but I really had no interest at all in reading a book of fiction. Rick saw right through my phony act and repeated, "Give it a try and see what you think."

I laughed. "Alright, alright, cool, I'll give it a shot."

Rick nodded and went on looking through the shelves.

Fiction wasn't my thing. It took me long enough to get into reading books on my own, but I felt like fiction was just a waste of time.

Soon after reading the first few chapters, I finally learned the true meaning behind never judging a book by its cover. I was all in. There were so many relatable details surrounding our communities that I found it hard to believe this book was a work of fiction. It took me four days to finish reading it, which was a record for me, and I couldn't wait to tell Rick my thoughts.

We met back in the library a few days later, and I was excited to tell Rick how impactful I thought the book was. I pulled up a chair across the table from him and started rambling about how the book took me on a journey through a hood I had never been to. Rick listened for a while, looked me straight in the eye, and asked, "What did you learn about yourself?"

"About myself?" I wondered. "I didn't. I mean, what was I supposed to learn about myself?"

"How to be a leader, for starters."

"Ah, yeah, I got that part."

Rick looked at me, shaking his head. "You know, you remind me a lot of myself. You're a good kid, but you have no leadership. I'm not here to preach to you, but what I've learned in my twenty years being locked up is being a follower is for suckers. I've seen you around, and people talk.

You have a good heart, but you have weak impulses. And if you're not careful, you'll end up right back in here, and every time you come back, it will be a different experience. Some are worse than others."

I nodded in agreement and thought about how lucky I'd been not to have had some of the experiences I'd witnessed other inmates have.

"What are you in here for?" I asked.

Rick drifted off as if he had gone back to the day his mistake had forever changed his life. He took a deep breath and said, "I went on a run I had no business going on. Two of my friends decided to rob a liquor store, and I was just hanging out with them. Shit went left, and the store clerk pulled out a gun. He was an older man, and his nerves got the best of him. He dropped the gun, and the next thing I knew, I was standing over him with a smoking gun and his head blown out all over my shoes. It was just that fast—my first run. My first time ever holding a gun." We were both quiet for a moment. "The point is, I was a follower. I never had any intentions of killing anyone, but when you're a follower, you have no control over the outcome."

That was the start and foundation of Rick's and my friendship. As it got closer to my release, our conversations about life, leadership, and accountability got deeper—so deep that one day, I told him that he sometimes reminded me of my pops or, more so, what I thought our conversations could have been if I had the chance to meet him. Rick, a man of few words, somehow always had a loaded question waiting on the tip of his tongue. "I hear you, Slim. I'm just trying to right my wrongs however I can, but here's a question: When was the last time you called home just to tell your mother you love her?" There was a deafening silence.

"Call her. Tell your momma you love her." I sat back and took notice of my childlike resistance. "You do love her, don't you?" Rick asked, leaning in.

"Yeah, man, of course I do."

"But . . . ?"

"But nothing, we're cool."

"Look, Slim, a lot of us take our pain out on the people we are closest to. Sometimes, we don't even realize the resentment we may have is because we are more similar to them and their ways than we think we are. The reflection of ourselves is sometimes hard to accept when we are not happy with who we've allowed ourselves to become. But you have to remember that we are all just doing the best we can from what cloth we're made of and where we come from. Who are we to pray for redemption if we don't allow the shortcomings of our own family and friends to be redeemed?"

That was my last conversation with Rick before he was transferred to another facility just days before my release. If those were the last words he'd ever say to me, I was okay with that because those were the most important and impactful words spoken to me at a moment when I most needed them. I walked away from that table with new mental tools I needed to see things from a different perspective. I replayed our conversation several times before getting up the courage to say those not-so-simple three words. I had told my mother I loved her many times, but this time would be intentional, not just something you say when you're leaving the house or hanging up the phone. Something that was a routine had a new meaning because I had gained insight into areas of my life that I wasn't aware of.

There was no better time to get the ball rolling on my new life. I was going home soon, and my only option was starting on the right foot. I waited nervously for my allotted fifteen-minute call. A few guys were ahead of me using the phones, so I listened in to hear how their calls with loved ones went. One guy was obviously on the phone with his wife; he dropped the words "baby," "honey," and "sweetheart" with every other sentence. He noticed me leaning in, so he signaled me with his finger to say give him a couple more minutes. "Okay, baby, other people are waiting to make a call. I'll call you next Sunday; I love you more." He wiped the phone with his shirt before hanging up, nodding and saying, "The phone is all yours."

Cleaning the phone with whatever you had on you—a shirt, a rag, or a napkin—was a way of keeping things cordial. I was leaning in so close he might've thought I was pressing him for phone time. The only thing I was pressing for was an example of a man's confidence while being vulnerable. I listened to the guy's call beside me as I slowly keyed in my code. "Okay, Ma. See you on the visit. Love you too." I noticed both calls ended with love in response to the woman on the other end of the line initiating it. I knew that wouldn't be the case for me, not this time.

Click. Click. The inmate phones clicked while waiting for the automated voice to signal that someone had answered the phone.

"You have a collect call from"—*beep*—"WallyGator, your son," I said when it was time to record my name. "This call is coming from SCI Dallas State Prison. Press the pound sign to accept this call."

Beep. She answered.

"Hey Jackie, how you be?" I said upbeat.

"What's wrong, Wallace? You okay?" she said right out the gate.

"Yeah, why?"

"I don't know, you sound funny, like something's wrong."

I wasn't sure if she could tell when something was wrong or different about me as quickly as she always did, or if she was just programmed to prepare herself for the worst-case scenario. I guess getting warmed up by a robotic voice reminding you every time we speak that I am calling from a fucking prison would set off some alarms.

"I'm cool. I'll be home in a couple of days and watch what I'm going to do."

"Oh yeah? Okay, Wally, that sounds good. I just got back from the store; you wouldn't believe how high they're marking up this food. I got to go to two or three different stores chasing the sales."

My chest tightened; anger, resentment, and neglect all started to bubble underneath its surface. My mother kept talking about her week at full steam like a train that just pulled out of its station. She never paused to ask what I would do. She never gave me more than a second to entertain my next moves. It hurt as usual. Her voice turned into a single hum of words I couldn't wrap my mind around. Rick's last words to me blanketed my rumbling emotions, and I recalled him telling me that she was only doing her best. Maybe she was afraid to be disappointed by more false hopes and promises. Maybe if she blocked me and everyone else out, making everything seem like it was always about her, she wouldn't give anyone the room to trespass into her heart and hurt her. Tears flooded my eyes, reflecting parts of me that were like hers.

"Well, okay, Wally, it was good talking to you," she said, although I hadn't said more than a few words in the ten minutes that passed.

Beep—"You have five more minutes," the recording interrupted. It was now or never.

"Ma . . ."

"What?"

"I love you."

For the first time in my life, I realized that more can be said in stretches of silence than anytime else.

"Okay, love ya too."

With four minutes left, we both paused just long enough to exhale. I hung up without saying goodbye. I could feel my heart still pounding in my throat. I knew we both had so much work to do on ourselves.

THE DAY HAD FINALLY COME. I was being loaded onto the prison transport van to be dropped off by the prison staff at the Greyhound station in Scranton, Pennsylvania. You may be wondering how things were leading up to my departure. I could tell you this: There is no farewell party, no warm brotherly daps or hugs, no going-home souvenirs, none of that. It's as painfully awkward and layered with uncertainty as the day you're first brought in. Smiles mask the jealousy of men wishing you never make it on the bus, or worse, they pray for the day you get brought back in.

Thankfully, those weren't my problems to dodge anymore. The ride to the station was short and came to an end with the first door to my freedom opened on the van.

"Alright, this is it. This is your stop. See you next month," the driver sarcastically said as the transport officer walked down the aisle, uncuffing the three of us and finally releasing us. That was our first test. I've heard of some men not making it off the bus before getting arrested for assaulting an officer who was shit-talking and provoking them before the ride was over. Some just don't know what they would do without the shackles of the institution. But not me. I'd dreamt of this day, and there was nothing that would come between me and my favorite lady, Freedom.

The pay phones inside the bus terminal took quarters, which I didn't have to make a phone call. An older man who was a porter approached me, jingling change in his pocket, and handed me fifty cents. He said, "Here ya go, man."

"Thank you. How'd you know?" I said, feeling a little embarrassed.

"I've seen fellas come and go; just make sure you make this one your last go," he replied with a smile.

"Trust me, never again."

I hurried to that pay phone, dropped a quarter in the slot, and listened excitedly to the phone ringing instead of clicking with an automated system.

"Yo," Steven answered the phone.

"Meet me at the downtown Philly station in three hours, dog. I'm coming home."

It was October 2001.

HALFWAY HOUSE

AFTER GETTING RELEASED EARLY FROM my original sentence at SCI Dallas, where twenty percent of the guys are in for life, I felt better than James Brown with a brand-new pair of patent leather shoes. I was released to a halfway house, and the most important thing for me was to stay out of prison—which meant my girl at the time, DeDe. She was a childhood friend from the neighborhood right around the corner, Thirteenth and Allegheny. For about a year before my release, she wrote me letters, sent me money, and visited me.

At the halfway house, they had a policy where the residents had to stay inside for a certain number of days before you got to go out. I wasn't tripping about it. People from around town would visit me to bring me food and clothes, and when I finally got to go out, I was only about fifteen minutes from my Nanny's crib. But DeDe was the main one. During the time I was in the halfway house, my relationship with DeDe got serious.

One day in mid-June 2002, while I was still in the halfway house, DeDe dropped off a copy of *Life and Def: Sex, Drugs, Money, + God* by Russell Simmons. At the time, I was serious about changing the trajectory of my life, looking at music as a legitimate avenue to transition from the streets. At the time, I had very few tangible models for what this transition meant, so Simmons's story served as inspiration.

After dropping off the book, DeDe called and I thanked her for the gift.

"I love you."

"*We* love you, too."

I moved the receiver from my face.

Who the fuck is we?

Returning the receiver to my face, I heard DeDe's playful laughter.

"Who the fuck is *we*?"

"The other one I'm carrying, crazy."

I wish I could remember how I responded to DeDe in that moment, but the exhilaration of hearing that I would be a father was immediately overshadowed by terror. Here I was, just shy of twenty-three years old, with almost half that time spent in the revolving door of juvenile and adult detention and correctional facilities, about to be a father. Nothing would've made me prouder than being a father at the time, to give a child the love and guidance that I didn't have. But when I thought about what I could give, I felt my heart clench. *How could I teach a child to be better than me when I haven't even figured out what that looks like for myself?* Though I would later convince DeDe that bringing a child into this world wasn't the best idea, in that moment I half entertained the thought of being a father—and figured my dreams of being a rapper would have to take a back seat to getting money the fastest way I knew how.

Though at the time I didn't allow myself to feel the loss of the unborn child, what really hurt me was seeing that I was already on a path similar to my father's, meaning my child would one day be on the same path as me. While I was proud of the stories I had of my father, I would trade all that legend and myth for the man himself. And knowing that there was no better legacy for a child than being present, that I wasn't in a place in my life to guarantee my own presence in my child's life is a pain that I wasn't prepared to deal with.

Just a few weeks later, I was out with the homies playing craps. In addition to the mixtapes, I was moving with the rap group Major Figgas and selling their T-shirts. My thought was I could scrape up some extra ends. That didn't happen. I went in looking to bust heads with the dice, and got my head busted instead. Between the slow build of getting buzz for my rapping, what I thought would be the inevitable arrival of a child, and my mentality at that time which refused to take an L, I sought to change my fate as quickly as it was made. In my mind the robbery would help me recoup the loss of the dice game, but I ended up losing way more.

SEPTEMBER 12, 2002

COMMONWEALTH OF PENNSYLVANIA
COUNTY OF PHILADELPHIA

On 7-19-02 at approx. 3:15 PM (2) B/M later
identified as Steven Peeples 28/B/M dob 3-17-74
& Wallace Peeples 23/B/M dob 6-21-79 entered the
Blockbuster store. Steven Peeples stood at the
front counter. Wallace Peeples walked to the rear
of the store and approached the store manager, then
produced a black handgun. The manager was walked
to the front of the store & behind the counter he
was ordered at gunpoint to open the safe. Defendant
Steven Peeples continued to stand at the front
counter telling several customers "calm down, ain't
nobody going to get hurt, ain't nobody leaving."
Taken from the store safe was approx. $1,100 USD.

The defendants fled the location then ran to a green
2-dr, 1997 GMC Yukon. This vehicle was parked in
front of 4342 N. Carlisle St. Both males got into
the vehicle then immediately "hid down" in the
front & back passenger seat. The vehicle fled the
scene NB on Carlisle St., EB on St. Luke, NB on
Broad St., then WB on Cayuga St.

Following flash information from responding police
officers to Blockbuster, the vehicle was observed
traveling WB on Armat St. by an unmarked SEPTA
police unit.

"GO, GO, GO!" I YELLED, running back to Larry's green 1997 Yukon, hopping into the passenger seat, and ducking down. Before I could even close the door, Larry slammed his foot on the gas. As he peeled out onto Carlisle Street, the tires screeched and left the stench of burnt rubber behind us. Steven was already on the floor in the back seat, repeating, "What happened, dog? Did you snatch something?"

"Man, let's just get back to the crib!"

We circled the area around Larry's house to make sure no one was following us before we parked. The coast was clear, so we parked the truck about half a block away, just in case. Paranoid, I looked back and forth out the four windows.

"What happened, man? You were just supposed to go in there and check the scene out," Larry demanded.

"I was, but they were watching me like a hawk the second I got in there."

"They? So what happened? What did you get?" Steven asked from the back seat, now sitting up practically in my face.

"Man, I went in and looked around for a few; the girl was at the register like you said she was. So, I was like, *Fuck it, this shit looks sweet; let me just tuck my hand under my shirt and make the jawn think I had a piece on me and have her clear out the cash drawer*," I said, pausing to drape my red scarf over my face and recline my seat. Even with my eyes covered, I could still feel Larry and Steven burning a hole through me with their eyes, waiting for me to detail how it went and how much we collected.

"So what's up? What did you get?" Steven urged.

"Hold up, let me finish. When I was about to walk up to the shorty at the register, this buff nigga came out from the back. I was like, *Oh shit, I thought homegirl was working the store alone*. Man, the dude was diesel and was sizing me up, so I just got up out of there 'cause I could tell they were about to call them boys on me."

The silence in the car was deafening. It was so quiet that I peeled off my scarf to read their facial expressions and convincingly finish telling them lies. I mean, there really was another worker in there that Larry never mentioned, but he wasn't buff at all; he actually wasn't even bigger than I was. The truth is, he was trying to be helpful and find a DVD I asked for, but that wouldn't help me sell my narrative to the guys. At the end of the day, there was no way I was going back to prison for making the same mistake. I had already been in and out of prison for the last five years.

Larry and Steven busted out in a roar of laughter.

"Yoooooo! Who are you talking about? The little dark, skinny nigga with the fucked-up hairline?" Larry cried out, laughing.

Damn, how'd he know?

"Man, I don't know about all that. All I knew was that he came out of nowhere and looked like he had Five-O on speed dial, and I wasn't about to wait around and find out. Besides, you said there was only supposed to be one female working in there. I could've gotten jammed up."

Larry and Steven didn't let up with the jokes and sarcasm at how I dropped the ball over something that was supposed to be a cake-walk. It didn't bother me for a second that I was being called every name in the book. I was the one who spent nearly the last five years in prison; getting roasted by my boys was a whole lot safer than not knowing whether you would be shanked in your sleep or not. It was all fun and games, snapping and clowning, until Larry pulled off without saying a word.

"Hold up! Where are we going now?" I sat up to ask, but Larry kept driving and didn't bother to answer. He looked back at Steven through the rearview mirror.

"Pass me the hammer. I got this. You got to stop playing, Wallo," Steven added. "I told you that baby ain't gonna feed itself."

I looked back at Stevie, replaying how I had only told him about DeDe and the baby, and now the information shared in confidence was being used to persuade me to commit another crime, therefore risking another prison sentence.

As Larry pulled up in front of the Blockbuster, I reached back and grabbed the gun from Steven. I couldn't find it in me to let anyone down, not even myself. Not this time. The cold metal of its handle sent a shiver down my spine.

"I got this! Let's go, Stevie! Keep the truck in drive, Larry, and stay on point!"

Both guys had a look of surprise on their faces, but I couldn't risk them going in there and dropping the ball and having to suffer the consequences. The last option I foolishly thought I had was to go in and get it done myself to lessen the risk. In and out like I used to, this time a little smarter and quicker. I knew in my heart that after I pulled this last route, I would never get caught up in anything like this again. I hopped out of the truck, shoving the SIG Pro .357 under my white T-shirt.

"Yo. You got that Denzel movie that came out a couple of years ago?" I asked the slim cat from earlier.

"Umm, I think that's *Remember the Titans*, right?"

"Yeah."

"Okay, yeah, that's right over here." As soon as he turned around to pull the DVD from the shelf, I shoved the gun into his back. "Be cool, and I won't hurt you. I need everything in the register real quick." While Steven kept a lookout by the door, I walked him back toward the counter. I shook my head at the girl at the register as a warning that she better not scream or move.

"More money. Get down and open that safe. I need it all! And you," I yelled at the scared girl, "go back there and get me the tape from today's date. Don't play!"

We ran out, straight back to the truck. Larry took off just like I told him. By the weight of the money, I could tell we didn't have more than a thousand dollars. But I had the surveillance tape; that's what really mattered. Speeding, we turned left on Carlisle, right on St. Luke, and left back onto Broad Street down to Cayuga. I felt a rush come over me. Not because I was thrilled to be back on route but because we got away. This was it! The last one. Never again. I was at peace knowing I was checking out of the game while whipping and whirling through the back streets of Philadelphia until the sound of police sirens blaring came from behind us.

"Oh shit. Go, go, go!"

No more than two to three minutes later, the truck slammed into a row of parked cars, and we had no choice but to take off running down the block on foot. It was every man for himself in this moment. Stevie must've turned in another direction because I no longer saw him in my peripheral vision. Cops were coming from everywhere. Larry and I ran into the house of a woman we saw standing on her porch, and she immediately screamed for us to get out of her home. I begged her to stay quiet. We just need to lay low for a few. But the minute the squad cars came speeding down her block, she screamed.

"They're here in my house!"

Larry fled upstairs, and I ran to the back, snatching the screen of the poor woman's window and breaking her cabinet off the wall, jumping out to run across her backyard. But it was too late. I jumped right in front of an officer who already had his gun drawn and aimed at my face.

The sound of handcuffs clicking behind me felt like a punch to the gut. I could hear the woman screaming inside, echoing down the alleyway. I knew Larry was caught too, but I wasn't sure about Stevie until the officers brought me around the corner, where all three of us were forced to sit on the curb in front of a gathering crowd.

About an hour had passed before witnesses from the Blockbuster were escorted to the scene, where they identified us as the robbers. Police officers were poking through, eyeballing bags of evidence pulled from Larry's truck—rounds of ammunition and bags of cocaine. Shit. I didn't even know those were in there, but it didn't matter. In the eyes of the law, it belonged to all of us. And I would be the one to take the worst fall.

I had been out of prison for only nine months.

IN THE COURT OF COMMON PLEAS OF PHILADELPHIA COUNTY

FIRST JUDICIAL DISTRICT OF PENNSYLVANIA

CRIMINAL TRIAL DIVISION

COMMONWEALTH   FEBRUARY TERM, 2003

VS

STEVEN PEEPLES NO. 0520

COMMONWEALTH   MARCH TERM, 2003

VS

WALLACE PEEPLES NO. 0144

FEBRUARY 20, 2004

COURTROOM 808

CRIMINAL JUSTICE CENTER

PHILADELPHIA, PENNSYLVANIA

BEFORE: HONORABLE SHELLEY ROBINS-NEW

APPEARANCES:

KALIOPE AGELAKIS, ESQUIRE

ASSISTANT DISTRICT ATTORNEY

FOR THE COMMONWEALTH

JOEL KRANTZ, ESQUIRE

PUBLIC DEFENDER

FOR THE DEFENDANT STEVEN PEEPLES

KATHLEEN MARTIN, ESQUIRE

FOR THE DEFENDANT WALLACE PEEPLES

SENTENCING VOLUME I

FEBRUARY 20, 2004

THE COURT: Mr. Wallace Peeples, would you stand
with your attorney. The court, Mr. Peeples, has
reviewed my notes in regard to the testimony
in this case. I've gone very carefully over the
presentence and the psych report and I have weighed
very closely and carefully what your counsel has
said and taken into consideration your family who
is here today.

I also find that the commonwealth has met its burden

to establish that this is a second-strike incident, having moved in and accepted the quarter sessions file in regard to the sentence from Judge Legrome Davis.

The court also considers the fact that this crime of violence occurred while you were basically at a halfway house as part of your parole while you were under Judge Davis's sentence.

The court therefore, on the crime of robbery as a felony of the first-degree, sentences you to ten to 20 years in prison.

On the charge of possessing instruments of a crime, the court sentences you to three-and-a-half to seven years to run consecutive to the ten to 20 years. In regards to one—excuse me, I apologize. I said that incorrectly.

On conspiracy, the court sentences the defendant to three-and-a-half to seven years to run consecutively.

On the charge of possessing instruments of a crime, the court sentences the defendant to one to two years in custody to run concurrent to all other sentences.

And on 6105, the court sentences the defendant to five to ten years to also run concurrent.

So the total maximum sentence for the defendant in this case would be 13-and-a-half to 27 years to run consecutive to the sentence he's presently serving from Judge Davis.

The court must impose mandatory court costs of $233.50. The court waives all supervision fees, and I would ask you to advise your client at this time . . . Mr. Peeples, you've just been sentenced. Do you understand what we're doing here today?

DEFENDANT WALLACE PEEPLES: I got a couple things to say. All my life I've been in jail. I think it

was before 11 that I was in jail. I'm 24. I got 12
years in institutions.

Now, Legrome Davis said that I just took on a chain
of time and that it's because I done the crime. All
my life I've been doing time. It's sad to say, time
is like you all done program me, you just hit me
with this. I don't even feel that 13 years that you
just gave me.

I don't even know my mom like that. You done
program me all my life. You all raised me. You all
my mother and my father, and you just give me these
13 years regardless of what she even said, and then
she bring the fact that what Legrome Davis say this
and say that.

It's not about change for me. It's just about him
throwing me away.

THE COURT: Mr. Peeples, I certainly understand
that feeling and I will tell you that not only did
the court consider that, but I think that it—at
a certain point, Mr. Peeples, though all of the
things that you say are probably correct, you also
have an opportunity to use and it's a long time—
I'm not going to say it's not a long time or it's
not going to be difficult, but when you come out,
you will be an adult who hopefully will be able to
function in society with whatever skills you choose
to learn in prison.

But Mr. Peeples, there comes a time when the law
sentences that are required are those which this
court must impose. I believe, just as Ms. Martin
said, we would all like you to have different
opportunities. You are clearly an intelligent
individual. You made certain choices, there may
have been many factors for which none of us
could control. And I do not have an answer for a
perfect system, though I certainly understand your

position, Mr. Peeples.

And the court absolutely considered those things in regards to the sentence that I chose to impose.

DEFENDANT WALLACE PEEPLES: Well, Your Honor, it's like, you know, like I told you, I don't even feel as though I'm going to do this time because I feel as though I'm going to get this overturned because I feel the trial was crazy. I didn't do this, Your Honor.

Like I told you, time is nothing to me. I already did 12 years. I've been doing this laying back. You've sent me here saying this is going to change. When I was 17, you sent me to the penitentiary. You put me with gorillas, with vicious gangsters. I'm a kid. "No, f- him, ship him up there, send him to Dallas Penitentiary where every day somebody gets raped and stabbed."

It ain't about me no more. It's about shoving him away.

I did not do this crime. If I did it I would have come in here and pled guilty and done the time. I never went to trial. When I'm wrong and wrong . . . The officers got on there, he laughed. This guy lied to my face, they personified, every one of them that got on there. They vicious.

THE COURT: Mr. Peeples, those will all be issues that you can bring up with your new counsel. I wish you good luck.

DEFENDANT WALLACE PEEPLES: You have a nice day. I'm not upset or none of that. Like the great governor of California, I'll be back. I'm going to send you a card, too, when I get home. Might even take you out to lunch.

(hearing concluded)

WHOEVER SAID CRIME DOESN'T PAY wasn't fucking lying. When we got arrested in 2002, the minimum wage in Philadelphia was $5.15 an hour. The day Larry, Stevie, and I got caught for that Hollywood robbery, we had $859 split between the three of us. If you do the math, that's $286 per person. For a wage worker to make as much as we did for ten minutes of work, they'd have to work fifty-five and a half hours. Pretty good for a dishonest day's work. But this was *if* we got away. We didn't.

I served fifteen years for $286. Let's do the math on *that*. If we took a full-time schedule of forty hours and multiplied that by fifty weeks a year (we'll account for vacation), you'd get two thousand hours. If we multiply two thousand by fifteen, the number of years I served, we arrive at thirty thousand hours. Now divide the $286 by the thirty thousand hours I spent in the penitentiary, and I made $0.009 an hour. Less than a motherfucking penny. Crime might pay in the short term, but over time, it costs way more.

□ □ □

THE THING ABOUT GETTING THE amount of time I received is that you must be grateful. Here's why: My first big sentence was in 1996 for the robbery of the Kentucky Fried Chicken. At the time, I was seventeen, and so used to playing the juvenile system that I thought I might do the same amount of time I was accustomed to doing.

Now, jail and prison are two different things. Jail is where you go *before* you're successfully tried and convicted of a crime. Prison is where you're sent *after* you're found guilty and sentenced. If freedom is heaven, jail is purgatory, and prison is hell. So, I was over in the wing for the young kids who were certified as adults. Every day I was there, somebody was getting sentenced, and listen, man, I remember one day a dude come back with life. Another dude got twenty to forty. So I literally went in my cell one day and just put my towel up and cried because I couldn't imagine at that time being off the street. I said to myself, *Man, I could do five, I could do six, but all this, I can't do it.*

So, when I got my time for the armed robbery, there was so much running through my mind. I was twenty percent appreciative, twenty percent sad, and sixty percent scared to death. I was appreciative because everybody else, most of them dudes that was coming back from court, they were hit with *way* more time than that. And then I was listening to all these younger dudes my age who are self-appointed experts and jailhouse lawyers.

"Yeah, they're probably going to give you twelve and a half to twenty-five."

The dehumanization of Black people in this country is such that we try to present as if pain doesn't hurt. So, I prepared myself while I was on the bus back to the jail from the courthouse. I was preparing myself like my face ain't up when I walk on the block.

"It ain't nothing man, they gave me twenty-seven years," I said.

I was telling people I was leaving with the back number. So I got in my cell and I was trying to figure out this fucking fear. This shit real.

MRS. OFFICER

FIVE YEARS INTO MY SENTENCE, I was in the yard walking around the track when this new female C.O. came up to me and told me that her cousin, a friend from the neighborhood, told her that I was here and to tell me what up. Because kindness in prison is rare, you notice it. And in noticing it, I realized that this C.O. was pretty, with a thick frame, five six, with skin the color of Starbucks caramel coffee. So I returned the kindness by being friendly, telling her what to look out for, which inmates to be careful around, how the prison worked. A kindness for a kindness.

Those exchanges went on for a few weeks until we were in the yard and she stopped me.

"I'm going to give you this address for you to write me."

All she gave me was the address. Because I didn't want to blow up her spot or mine, I memorized it on the spot and threw the paper away. With all the years I had behind bars, I had a lot of practice writing love letters. So, I wrote her a first letter that was low-key. Like a teenager experiencing puppy love, I was just sharing innocent feelings of attraction with her—how beautiful I thought she was, how I wish I could take her on a date to her favorite restaurant, all the shit you might read in a Terry McMillan novel. I was keeping the real gentleman first.

When she wrote back, she seemed more eager to get past the formalities and for me to tell her what I really wanted to do. That was all I needed to hear. I went and wrote a cold-blooded smut letter that would make Zane jealous. I wrote this letter called "Imagine This."

IMAGINE THIS . . .

It's the middle of the night and you opened my cell up. You came in the cell and being as though you knew we didn't have a lot of time, I kissed on you immediately. You took your uniform off. After you took the uniform off, I put you on your knees and you show me how your lips felt. Then I put you over the bed and returned the favor, pleasuring you from the back until you woke the entire prison up . . .

After she read that letter she wrote me back, saying, *Every time I see you, my body melts.* She was turned on by my ability to entice her imagination. I'm not celebrating prison, and I don't believe you have to go to prison to learn this, but when you're free, as a man, we have all the ways of attracting women that exist outside of us—money, jewelry, expensive dates. But when you're incarcerated, you don't have any of that; you have your mind and your ability to create a picture that needs to feel as real as the outside.

A few weeks later I was down in the kitchen and she wound up being one of the guards to come and be the security there that day. Being one of the top cooks in the prison, I had some privileges of relative trust and freedom. My man Psycho was down there chilling, and I headed to one of the shelves by where she was, pretending that I was looking for something, and then I whispered to her about one of the blind spots in the prison. Because this was an old penitentiary, there were so many blind spots where the cameras couldn't see. A lot of us learned to see where the cameras couldn't, and we finessed the gray areas.

A lot of times people will stem for you. Stemming is when someone you trust in prison creates a distraction for you to do what you need to before someone catches on. So as Psycho stemmed for me, she and I went to a storage closet. First, she went in, then I lagged and pretended like I was looking for something and slid in behind her. As soon as I slid in, I started kissing her, squeezing her ass. I'm grabbing her by the neck, putting my tongue in her mouth. Though it feels good to experience the physical touch of a woman, someone soft, I didn't want us to get caught because first and foremost, nothing was more important to me than her job security. I couldn't let her get caught up. So what really felt like an eternity of passionate kissing was really two minutes in this tight-ass storage closet.

During her shift a few days later, I see her again in the yard and she tells me she has a number for me for a cell phone that's not under her name.

"What you mean?" I asked her.

"The days I work when I'm here aren't enough. I need to be talking to you."

I put the number on my phone list, which is a registry of all the people you call that must be approved by the prison. For people who might think, *Well, wouldn't the prison monitor the calls?* That's really some shit you see on television. If you're a high-profile drug trafficker or kingpin, maybe, but for the average inmate, once the call sounds like some boo-loving, there's really no reason to be that deep. You must think about the budget the state would need to have two thousand inmates have their conversations monitored by correctional officers. It's just not realistic.

Over the next month, we talked on the phone about what we'd do to each other if we had more time, and where I'd take her when I got out, and the things I'd do to her sexually the next time I saw her. All she kept saying to me was, "I can't wait till you come home." In prison, the "come home" was our slang for that storage closet, and we were plotting on how we'd have more time than we did before to have sex. By the next time I saw her I felt like that song "Love You Down" by Ready for the World. I was totally in my zone.

That day, Psycho and I were on the same kitchen detail, and she was already in the closet waiting. As soon as I walked through the door, she unbuckled her belt and pulled her pants down to her ankles like they were on fire and bent herself over the boxes. Harder than a fucking bag of nickels, I slid into her like I was at a water park. For five and a half strokes, I felt like a free man.

Over the two years of our relationship, we probably had sex four times. But them times were so powerful it kept us going strong. But one day her energy shifted. She was no longer taking my calls or returning my letters. Whereas before when we'd see each other, we'd find our way to each other, now she seemed to always be out of reach. Without being able to explain it, I knew she must've been dealing with someone on the outside. No matter what I gave her when she was here, at the end of the day, she could go where I couldn't and that was out this motherfucker.

DEAR FREEDOM,

Let's jump right into it. Over the past four years, I've thought about writing you every single day, but I couldn't find the courage to face you. I was ashamed, embarrassed, and angry that I had betrayed you. If it means anything to you, I realize I betrayed the people I love, and losing you was the most ruthless consequence. I didn't think I was worthy of addressing you for a long time, and it hurt. But I've come around to a clearer perspective on life and my growth and accountability, and I wanted you to know that I'm giving it all I got! I am not asking you to forgive me. Shit, I'm still working toward forgiving myself.

Anyway, I will keep this short and slowly but surely prove that my actions will speak louder than my words. I am a changed man now, Freedom. You have my word, for whatever it's worth! And while I would love to hold you again, I know that all things happen for a reason, and our time will surely come.

I'm out.
Wallo

□ □ □

TIME HAS A WAY OF humbling the beast in you. Even the most ravenous of appetites can be calmed in time. For me, time has been relentless in unraveling the tangled web of delusion I held on tightly to. Time became my silent teacher by replacing my arrogance with accountability. It sounds strange, but after a short while, I realized that my second bid in prison was meant to allow me the time to re-fine the man I started to become right before my early release. I hate to say it, but I wasn't mentally ready to stand on my own two feet as a man in the free world and apply the knowledge I learned from my first go-round in the penitentiary. But it took time for me to under-stand that: time and humility.

I remember the day I learned the word *ravenous*; it was one of the first words my pointer finger landed on as I randomly flipped the dic-tionary pages in the law section of the library, looking to broaden my vocabulary. Thumbing through the dictionary and law books was one of the activities the old heads would always preach the importance of to me. Building my arsenal of words was just one of the practices I promised myself I would improve on while I served my time. Part of the challenge was to find three words that begin with the same letter and start applying them to daily conversations. *Reflect* and *redemption* were the two other words that seemingly jumped off the pages need-ing my attention.

This small challenge forced me to use the word *reflect* in more than just conversation, but to utilize it in my life and make it work for me somehow. I thought about what it meant to reflect on my life hon-estly; that was the first time I saw my true self in the mirror. I allowed myself to reflect on parts I had neglected for the greater part of my life. There were rotten layers I had never seen festering inside of me.

Years of anger, bitterness, and self-righteous victimization that I had no idea existed were brewing inside me like a volcano ready to erupt.

For the first time in my life, there was no mask to cover the destructive and irrational denial I had of myself. No disguise was left to distract me from the pain and anguish I caused others. I committed thoughtless crimes under the false idea that good intentions were enough to justify doing terrible things. I had so many excuses and reasons why what I was doing on those streets wasn't as bad as everyone made it out to be. *Oh, I'm so generous. I give most of my gains back to the hood, so I'm good. Oh, I was never going to use the gun on anyone. I'm not robbing them personally; I'm robbing multimillion-dollar companies. Oh, and even when I did jack someone personally, it was quick and easy, and no one was hurt.*

I spent years covering up my misdeeds by justifying them with what I felt were valid grounds to do whatever I wanted. I hid behind the veil of being a follower, yet I took the lead on every route I took. I pointed guns in the faces of women and men, some young and some old, not once thinking about how traumatizing that could have been for them. Someone could have died by my hand, including myself, and the realization of all these things came crashing down on me like a ton of bricks the moment I took the time to truly self-reflect.

Growth and maturity didn't come overnight or easily. It was a long and painful process of peeling back the layers of the reckless tyrant I'd allowed myself to become. There wasn't anywhere or anyone to turn to amid the daily chaos and madness that took place within the caged hell called a prison cell. Officers and staff were only vested in their own futures, and rehabilitation of career criminals would only disrupt the future of their job security. I had to do the work alone.

I CAME BACK FROM MY TRIAL in worse mental and emotional condition than I had ever been. I was a ball of fire and aggression. I was mad at the world and filled with rage. If the judge could have added years to my sentence for the way I exploded once hearing the guilty verdict, I probably would have never made it out of there.

"You'll see me again. Like the great governor of California says, 'I'll be back,'" I yelled at the judge while the officers dragged me, thrashing and cursing, back to my grim reality. It took several years of anger and resentment for me to finally get sick of myself. I had to forgive everyone. And most of all, I had to learn to forgive myself.

For six years into my bid, I was just focused on not wanting to be back in prison. Around 2008, I knew this time I was done. I'll never forget: It was the summer, and it was hotter than the hood of a Toyota in July. There was no air-conditioning in prison, so in addition to the air being hot, it was also thick with the smell of sweaty, musty grown-ass men. Everybody was in the yard, but I decided I wanted to be alone.

Trying to keep cool, I went to the sink in my cell to splash water on my face. As I was looking in the mirror, the thought hit me like a sock filled with bars of Dial soap: *What the fuck is the matter with me? I'm in prison for being somebody I'm not.* Because even when I was robbing and boosting, I had a conscience. I knew what I was doing was fucked up, but I was too afraid to accept that confronting the reality meant I had to change it, and I didn't know how. When you're at your lowest, life has a way of picking you up, and this is how I started watching Anthony Bourdain.

In prison, we inmates were allowed to buy televisions and a cable subscription with our commissary money. The TV would be installed in the inmate's cell, and we also had to buy headphones so we could listen without interfering with our cellmate. One of my favorite channels to watch when I bought a television and decided it was time to change my thinking was the Travel Channel because that was the only way for me to escape prison. *Parts Unknown, The Layover,* and *No Reservations* were shows that took me all over the world. The Travel Channel showed me different parts of the country, the best beaches, restaurants, and places to visit. Because I watched so many episodes, I can't recall certain episodes—they all feel like one long film. But the total effect of seeing the world beyond the prison walls and North Philly was inspiring.

Of all the things I *do* remember about specific episodes of the shows, what impacted me the most was when I learned that before Anthony Bourdain became this world-class chef who traveled the world, he was in New York City getting high. It changed me in a good way because it let me know the possibilities were endless. Sometimes being from our communities, the models we have for possibility are limited. Before I knew Bourdain's story, I focused on all the ways he and I were different. He was a white man who seemingly didn't come from the same world as me, and so I thought his life was easy. Then I learned about his struggles with addiction and realized that no matter who he spoke to, it never seemed like he thought he was better than anyone. He was just as curious about an everyday person as he was a diplomat. Knowing that I had the equal ability to make friends with anyone and talk to people from different backgrounds, I learned from Bourdain's shows that people who were good with other people and words, regardless of their past, had a future.

Another thing I became fascinated with were commercials, which at a point in my bid were the show. I would just turn on the television, waiting for shows to go to break. I remember one day watching a McDonald's commercial and seeing the way the patty laid on the bun with the lettuce looking crisp and the bun all soft and shit, and thinking, *My burger never looked like that.* I was somewhat aware of what marketing was at that time, so I knew this had something to do with it, but for some reason, that commercial inspired me to learn about the marketing game. And one of the greatest books I read in prison was George Lois's *Damn Good Advice (For People with Talent!): How to Unleash Your Creative Potential by America's Master Communicator.*

In the book, Lois, who ran some of the greatest marketing campaigns in history, breaks down these insights into how marketing and advertising works. One of the concepts I remember the most was "A Big Idea Can Change World Culture." To Lois, a Big Idea was an attempt to communicate a brand by creating a strong message that pushed brand boundaries and resonated with the people you were trying to reach. When I thought about how the hustlers in the hood would drive around in their Benz, blasting music and flashing jewelry and knots of hundred-dollar bills with the fine woman in the passenger seat, they were marketing and advertising their lifestyles. Even though the reality of the street life comes with way more than diamonds and Dom Pérignon, you can't attract people to your lifestyle by showing them everything. You have to show people what you want them to see, and what you know they want to see.

Thinking back to the neighborhood when the nine-to-fivers were being ignored while the hustlers were being celebrated, I realized that so much of my own path wasn't influenced by the reality of the streets but the way it was *marketed* to me. Reading that book made me see that what companies show us is all a game. This sparked a deeper curiosity in me and led me further down this rabbit hole of knowledge. Then I learned about Steve Stoute, who at the time had a book called *The Tanning of America: How Hip-Hop Created a Culture That Rewrote the Rules of the New Economy*. Stoute is a respected figure in the culture because he was able to understand the value of Black culture and translate that value to companies in order to have our experiences reflected on a broader scale. And ironically enough, Stoute was the mastermind who tapped Pusha T to write one of McDonald's catchiest slogans, "Ba da ba ba bah, I'm lovin it." While it might be crazy to think that a dude who raps about drugs could make one of the most successful and catchy jingles for one of the biggest companies in the world, anyone from the hood knows that when you're a hustler, the product might change but the hustle doesn't.

I began to shift my perspective and adopted a whole new mindset. I started to adjust my focus and approach my time left in prison as if it were Princeton. What was happening in the yard and the chow halls was no longer entertaining, and neither was it any of my concern. My cell became my classroom, and I was both teacher and student. I aimed for perfect attendance with a laser focus on becoming the man I longed to be. It was now or never, my past versus my future.

My Letters to Freedom took a back seat to my new form of writing. I started journaling daily stories, which I named "The Book of Life." Initially, the stories were about what was happening in my surroundings. I was intentional with the words I used, such as calling the men "men" as opposed to "inmates" or "prisoners." I wrote about several topics, one being the damage of isolation in the hole for extended periods of time and the psychosis it caused that would challenge even the strongest of men. I wrote about the sleep deprivation caused by men who used torture tactics such as screaming rage-fueled insanity until the sun came up or banging on steel toilet bowls like drums for hours to ensure no one got any sleep because their own demons didn't allow them to.

A few months into my newest writing form, I realized what was on the pages in front of me were the very things I wanted far behind me. There wasn't anything that could erase the haunting suffocation of years spent behind prison walls, but I knew writing about it would allow my true healing to begin.

"The Book of Life" was a series of blueprints that allowed me to work through my desire for change, and it transformed me in ways I could never have imagined. There weren't any rules or guidelines on how it was structured. The only commitment was to get it down on paper and be honest with my fears and intentions. From the moment I allowed myself the freedom to know what I wanted from life and how to command it, my mind opened to opportunities. I could write freely about what I wanted to achieve, about the goals and ideas I wanted to bring to life without fear of judgment or rejection. That was the ultimate game changer for me.

While I continued writing, I started to recognize I was struggling with some deep-seated emotions. With every step I took in my trans-formation, I faced one recurring obstacle: my relationship with my mother. I could remember her words clearly, like it was just yesterday, when I called her after my sentencing, and she said matter-of-factly, "You'll be alright." That wave of coldhearted dismissal ran through my body and felt like it would shatter every inch of me. Her words and the numbing feeling that came with them stayed frozen in time until I warmed up to the truth that my mother was a victim of my past too.

You don't go to prison alone. You don't even do the time alone. Believe it or not, the ones who love you are emotionally suspended in a mental cell right beside you. From the financial burden of obtaining lawyers, bail money, and commissary, to missing work to make court appearances, to the stress of sleepless nights, they are victimized and punished, too, by your crimes and poor decisions.

I realized I had been holding on to that moment for some years. While learning how to forgive, I should have also been learning how to be sincere in my apology for all the dysfunction I played a role in. I began to understand that the pain I'd caused her had to have been the catalyst for her heart growing cold. I knew that if I wanted to transform, this was one of the wounds I would have to learn to heal.

My cellmate, Shoe, advised me on many different ways to look at life. His perspectives allowed me to see things in unfamiliar ways. Ironically, Shoe was an OG who knew my father and had stories about him that helped. Shoe was a sickly man whose hands were spotted with age and disease. He would sometimes notice me staring at them and ball his weakening hands up, hiding them in shame. He was in a wheelchair and diagnosed with cancer, so I would push him around and listen to him.

"Don't worry about that, OG; I'm just in the zone, listening," I would say to comfort him and let him know we were in a safe space as he talked about his life experiences. We bunked together for some years as he slowly withered away from what we thought was cancer. In a sense, he was like a father figure.

Everything happens for a reason, and I'm sure being bunkies with Shoe was some form of divine intervention. Having an elder who came up in the same era as my father gave me the courage to sit through my fleeting thoughts and tap into my emotions. I could only imagine how chaotic things could have become if I had been paired with anyone half as angry and bitter as I was when I reentered the system. It wouldn't have taken much to ignite the hellfire that once burned in my heart. I know now that I needed to love and be loved. You won't hear those words from many men behind bars. Vulnerability is something we are deathly afraid of. But, if it weren't for the words of encouragement, wisdom, and love from Shoe, I would not have made it this far. Through him, I learned the true meaning of love and loss.

Shoe gradually grew sicker and was spending more and more time in the prison nursing stations and hospital rooms. The sight of his condition and the shattering of his once-hopeful spirit began to fracture my heart bit by bit. It was a double-edged sword, allowing light to seep into places in my heart that had long been blocked off, waiting for my father to fill them.

I would help him navigate his pain during the day by picking him up from the medical wing and getting him out in the yard for fresh air. Gradually, Shoe became too weak and preferred to stay in and rest as much as he could. That's when I started to check out extra books from the library to bring to our cell and read them aloud. This practice helped me further my reading skills, which were once below average, and made me more aware of my cadence and how I projected my voice. These skills would later be tools in my arsenal that I desperately needed to fulfill the self-prophecies I had written in "The Book of Life."

Shoe loved these gummies dusted in sugar called orange slices. Every time I went to commissary, I'd get him some and spend my rec time talking to him. It was the closest thing to a father-son relationship. One day in 2008, while I was sitting next to him, he grabbed my arm.

"Listen man," he said in a sharp tone. "When you go out, I need you to do me a favor."

"What you want me to do when I go to the yard?"

"I'm not talking about no damn yard," he shot back. "I'm talking about when you go home."

"What?"

"I spent my whole life in and out of these joints. I ain't never seen nothing. I ain't never go nowhere." He had a death grip on my arm. "Live your motherfucking life. Just do it for me."

"I'm going to do it," I told Shoe.

"You special, Wallo."

As much as I appreciated what he was telling me, I thought two things: Either this nigga crazy or he knew something I didn't. He was telling me I'm different when I'm serving another prison sentence for violating my pre-release.

The next day, while I was waiting for a guard to release Shoe from his hospital bed, a nurse suggested I return later or another day. I knew something had to be wrong, or his pain had taken a turn for the worse, but I held on to faith, knowing that Shoe was one of the strongest men I had ever known.

"No problem, miss. Just let him know I came by, and we got some good work to do." "Good work"—that's what we used to call our studies, journaling, and the random acts of kindness we encouraged each other to strive for.

I was excited to sit with Shoe that day because I finally got my hands on the "Purple Book." That's what we called Iyanla Vanzant's book *Acts of Faith* because it had a noticeable purple cover. This book had a long waiting list to get and quickly became one of the blocks' most traded books if you owned one. Even from a distance, you could tell who was working toward bettering themselves by the books they chose. Most guys who weren't ready for reform read books like *48 Laws of Power* and *"Yellow Kid" Weil: America's Master Swindler*. Those books were trendy but also known as the con man's bibles.

"The Purple Book" was one of the most influential books I've ever read, and I was excited to start reading it with Shoe. There were daily affirmations and inspirational messages that I knew we could put to use day by day as he was being nursed back to health. It would have given us something to look forward to and keep us grounded as our hours turned to days and days turned into years until freedom came to look for us.

I found out later that day Shoe had passed away from HIV-related complications the night before.

Grief can undo many things. Faith is one of them. With the terrible news, I felt my faith starting to buckle swiftly beneath me. All the "good work" we had done together started to feel purposeless. Grief slipped into shock, crashed into resentment, and, worst of all, collapsed into the isolation of daddy issues.

Shoe's last words calling me special became my lifeline, something tangible I could anchor myself with as I weathered the storm of my loss. After my initial loss of faith, I looked to God more than I had ever before. I prayed for a sign and a stabilizing force to keep me grounded and help me continue the good work we started. Nanny had always told me about the miracles that can only come through prayer, so I did just that. My prayers were a mix of Christianity, Islam, and Eastern spirituality. I needed a miracle fast.

A few weeks later, I was informed by an officer that my time alone in my cell was coming to an end and that I needed to prepare my cell for a new knucklehead cellmate. Little did we know my new cellmate was my brother Steven, who had just arrived on an inmate transfer from Pine Grove, where he was doing time.

Look at God!

One thing I could tell you is that I don't know if Steven's transfer to Dallas with me would count as a miracle, but God knew I needed something or someone to help keep me afloat. And seeing my brother's face after years of incarceration had to be the closest thing to a miracle I had ever experienced.

"Yoooo!"

"Oh shit. Yoooo!"

Those were the only words we could find between the laughter and tight hugs we gave each other. Unfortunately, this wasn't my first time locked up with a family member. Hip, Steven's father, had also been my cellmate for a few months just a few years before. It seemed like prison had a revolving door with a welcome mat for my friends and family.

Many things had changed since I'd been away: technology, cars, and styles, but many negative things had stayed the same. Steven still had a drug habit that was the underlying cause of the crimes he committed. When you have an itch for a fix, the only way to scratch it is to get your paper together and get it. Sometimes you'd get lucky on a route, and other times, you might be able to get it on credit. But everybody knows credit is the worst option, even when your funds are low. Most of the time, you wind up paying back way more than you actually owe. His drug addiction may have been the indirect cause of why I was in prison doing a whole new sentence. *What the fuck would make me think Steven was in the right frame of mind for me to go along with robbing a spot just a few months out of prison?* I would ask myself. But that question made me bitter and sometimes angry with Steven until I learned to take accountability for myself.

Over the next six months, Steven and I grew closer than we had ever been. We stayed up late nights, talking about life, our childhood, and all the ideas I had written in the "Book of Life" that would eventually help break the cycle our family was stuck in. To this day, I don't think anyone in this world believed in me more than Steven. He would watch me as I binged books, pacing the floor until an idea hit, and I would rush to get it written in my notebook.

"Boy, when you get out of here this time, you gonna make it big! Real big, I swear! You got a mean hustle about you, Wallo. You got more hustle than any of these niggas in here. If you never listened to anything I said, trust me, I know a star when I see one!" Steven said.

And I believed him.

MOMENTUM

21

THINGS STARTED LOOKING UP FOR me and Steven. We decided to enroll in the prison addiction program together so that I could be supportive of him and also learn how to cope with friends and family once I made it back out to the free world. The thing about those types of programs is that you don't have to be an addict to gain something from them. There is something to be said about being transparent about your shortcomings in a group setting where no one can judge another. I spoke about my past addiction to fast money as my reason for selling to people just like them. I would notice the looks of men who seemed to despise me for not ever having tried drugs yet benefited from their downfall.

Showing up consistently for weeks on end gave me a purpose. I learned to work through confrontation with people that I have indirectly hurt without ill intentions. Through open communication, I was able to address the many traumas in my life to the point where I was slowly able to forgive myself for the mistakes I made and let go of some of the grief I was still holding on to.

There was one particular young bul named Rico who was in the program, and you could tell he was still smacked out of his mind at times. It was obvious he was straddling the fence of addiction. One side wanted to get clean and graduate from the program, and the other had a firm hold on him. Steven didn't quite understand why I took an interest in Rico's rehabilitation. To be honest, Steven always was a certified hater. He hated everything and everyone that wasn't family, but with good reason. Trust issues played a huge role in how my brother perceived things, but he'd say that was his way of not leaving any room for anyone to fuck him over. He could call someone's bluff and profile them in under thirty-two seconds. That, too, was a skill learned as a con man. He was raw with his words and said exactly how he felt when he felt it, and whether it hurt your feelings or not, he couldn't care less. When I think of it, he was the complete opposite of me when we were younger because I did everything I could to be accepted by everyone.

One day, Rico came to our session about a minute or two before being locked out. They had strict rules on being punctual that had previously caused other men to fail out of the program when not kept. Rico was tall and lanky and had a little dirt mustache similar to the one I had when I first got sent to Dallas at seventeen. He reminded me of my younger self, which was one reason I felt compelled to help. He ignored an empty seat next to me, but I nodded at him to take it. Once Rico sat down, the drug prevention counselor started handing out papers with a writing assignment on each of them. I looked over at Steven, and he was already staring back at me with a look of disgust.

"Man, you need to worry about yourself!" Steven said in a low but aggressive tone.

"Chill, he's cool," I said, trying to keep Steven from causing a scene. The number one rule in prison is to mind your business and stay out of the way if you want to survive. My brother was just being protective and trying to keep me from picking up anyone else's baggage by association. Sometimes, even investing in someone else's well-being will set you up for failure.

"Alright, brothers, peace. There have been some rumblings around the blocks that this program isn't providing any real benefits and that many of you are just here to earn points and maybe get some time shaved off when you go up before the board. Now, while I understand wanting to play the best hand you can when the time comes for you to plead for your freedom, I can't say that it's not disheartening to hear such bad reviews of our program. *Dis-heart-en-ing.* If you're unfamiliar with that word, please write it at the top of your worksheet and look it up before next week. I, just like some of you, have spent years in and out of prisons. I am currently serving my twenty-fifth year of a life sentence without the chance of parole, so while I don't care about how you feel about me, I do care about what you feel about this program. I have dedicated my life to this program and several others, and it hasn't been easy to get approval for any of them," Joe Brown said.

Joe was the appointed drug program counselor. He wore brown-tinted glasses that matched his brown jumpsuit and his complexion. We used to say you couldn't tell from a distance where his face, neck, or torso began because it was one continuous shade. I'm unsure if Brown was his last name or something we made up as a joke.

Joe Brown took his glasses off, which was a rare occasion for anyone to witness. His eyes almost disappeared once the thick, goggle-like glasses stopped magnifying them. He rubbed his beady, watery eyes and wrinkled forehead, then let out a stress-filled sigh.

"You know what? Today I want to do something different. I will go around the group and allow each of you to address the man next to you and tell them what you think about their progress since starting this program five weeks ago and what changes you think they can make before we close out in week six. Let's keep it positive and respectful, please."

The room filled with sighs and nervous laughter after hearing about the assignment. A few guys shifted in their seats, and one anxiously rubbed his hands back and forth above his knees. Everyone reacted except Rico.

"Let's start with you, Peeples."

"Huh?" I replied, pointing to myself.

"That's right, let's start with you, Wallo. Please stand and start with the person to your left."

I cautiously stood, wringing my hands nervously. "Well, Rico, first, I'd like to thank you for attending today's session."

The group instantly began to laugh.

"Let him finish, guys!" Joe said as he put his Coke-bottle glasses back on. "Go on, Peeples."

"Well, like I said, thank you for being here today. Now, if I have to start by saying something positive, I would say you've consistently attended group, which has to count for something."

Rico interrupted me, mumbling under his breath, "Man, shut the fuck up."

The group burst into laughter again.

"Naw, it's cool," I said. "I could shut the fuck up, but honestly, it won't do either one of us any good." Rico pulled himself up from the slumped posture he was sitting in to look me in the eyes. "Look, I'm not gonna waste anyone's time here, mine or yours, 'cause if I'm being honest, you look like you're wasting your time on your own." By the movement in the room, it was clear that it grabbed everyone's attention, and they were ready for some sort of confrontation.

"Continue," Joe said as he quieted the room.

"I usually don't say stuff like this, but you remind me of myself when I was younger, and what's fucking me up is I didn't have my father around either, but the difference between you and me is that I don't have kids to break that cycle for. You do! I lost my blessing by getting locked up in here again. And no disrespect to you, but I've heard you talk about all the things you used to do and the man you were before the drugs, but why are you still holding on to that? Who gives a fuck about what it was? Not your kids, not your lady back home, none of that shit even matters anymore. That's the past! It's over! What are you going to do today to be a better man? To be a sober father? Because nobody gives a fuck about who you once were. That Rico is gone! Who will you be today for a better tomorrow?"

The strength of my words and the bass of my voice deepened with every syllable. The room was silent. I was speaking from my soul, and it wasn't just for Rico; it was for Steven too, to whom I never dared to say these words.

"Wow! Thank you, Peeples," Joe said as I took my seat and wiped a tear from my eye.

"Yeah. And it's just like that!" I concluded. Everyone broke into laughter again, brushing off the uncomfortable tension of vulnerability.

That was the day my life changed. From that moment, I knew what my purpose in this world was. I knew I could never right my past wrongs, but I knew I could help make a difference in the lives I touch moving forward. There was an energy that sparked inside me that I had never felt before.

"And it's just like that" became my signature sign-off anywhere I saw fit.

□ □ □

AFTER THE PRISON BOARD RECOMMENDED Steven for an intensive criminal rehabilitation program for six months, we got separated into different blocks for a few years, unable to see each other for a while. I took that time to gain several certificates and attend multiple programs. Anger management was one of the more interesting of them. We learned how to avoid explosive and unnecessary arguments through cognitive behavior therapy and de-escalation techniques—those are fancy words for knowing when and how to talk yourself off the ledge before punching somebody in the face. The more I attended sessions, the more I began to visualize myself as someone who could offer a hand in reform and rehabilitation inside and beyond prison walls.

"Usually, when people are sad, they don't do anything. They just cry over their condition. But when they get angry, they bring about a change." That is one of my favorite quotes from Malcolm X that I shared with the group. I wanted them to understand it was okay to be angry, but what you do with that anger is what matters the most.

As time went by, Steven and I were able to meet in the yard again. He had successfully completed his program and was in the process of getting his case appealed. We would bring each other different foods and snacks to share as we sat and discussed our future plans.

"I don't know what it is about you, Lo, but the people love you. You really got something special. Damn, I wish my lawyer could get you out of here too. But, I promise, I'm gonna tell everybody back home about how you're in here moving. I'm proud of you!" he said with excitement in his voice. I was just so happy to see my brother clean and sober, with ambition and ready to help me take over the world once we both made it back to freedom.

If I knew that day in the yard would be my last time seeing my brother, I would have held on to him tighter.

STEVEN'S LAWYER GOT HIS GUILTY verdict overturned a few days later and got him home on appeal.

You feel a roller coaster of emotions when your right hand, your brother, gets another chance at freedom but has to leave you behind until your time comes. Of course, you're excited for him, and you're happy that at least one of you gets out, but you're also faced with the grief of losing him while you stay stuck in the system. It could be challenging to navigate what you're feeling. It seems like the window of opportunity to express those feelings closes before you can process and understand them.

With all the books I'd read and programs I'd participated in, I still didn't have all the tools to recognize my selfish behaviors. Not long after Steven settled in back home, he and I got into a riff that broke down our communication for longer than it should have. Years, even.

I was selfish in thinking Steven was supposed to do whatever it took to get me out, too. Like he had needed for his attorney, I needed $5,000 to pay a lawyer to help me appeal my case. He felt the evidence was stacked against me and would be a waste of legal fees. And I felt like he chose to play the sidelines when it came to my legal battle. His absence in this fight felt like a betrayal; after all, I was here because of him and his bad idea.

Without any outside help, there wasn't much more I could do than turn my confinement into further opportunities. Amid steel bars, I found my silver lining and developed a passion for making gourmet meals with the humblest ingredients. With my reputation for being the nicest chef with potatoes, onions, and a few "borrowed" secret spices, word got around that earned me a promotional transfer to Graterford Penitentiary in 2009. Although Graterford was another maximum-security prison that I would have to figure out my way around, they hosted a culinary arts program, and I was ready for a new notch on my belt that could change the game.

When a transfer happens, you tell your people and this sets off a network of communication where if people in your circle know anyone at the prison you're being transferred to, they send a message ahead of your arrival to look out for when you touch down. This is how I connected with my old head Big Jake. Jake was a no-nonsense dude who was built like Arnold Schwarzenegger. Because his son's mother and my mother were cool, our connection was established.

When I got to Graterford, I enrolled in their culinary program, graduated, and got a job in the kitchen cooking for 5,000 inmates. Because of this job in the kitchen, I got time to do my own thing, making special food for the workers in the kitchen. I started this hustle where I sold platters—baked chicken, baked macaroni, fried fish, fried rice—for a pack of cigarettes, which amounted to $10. Big Jake became one of my customers. For two years, Big Jake was another old head who took me under his wing, made sure I didn't fly too close to the sun, and made sure I didn't drown.

One day I got on the phone with my mother.

"Wally, I have a story to tell you about Big Jake," she said.

This is when my mother told me that before she and my father began dating, she had a relationship with Big Jake's brother.

"One day I'm riding in the car with your father, and Big Jake's brother and his friends were standing on the corner, and Big Jake started shooting at our car."

Wait what?!

"Yeah, I was pregnant with you at the time."

What the fuck?!

In that moment, I was processing that this old head who was teaching me about life almost stopped me from having one. Though it may have been impulsive to want to do something to Big Jake, I didn't have the malice in my heart. I wasn't going to deactivate the brotherhood for something that happened in 1978. It was in that moment when I believed Shoe when he said I was special.

While at Graterford, I maintained the same amount of focus on my studies and self-improvement journey that I had started at Dallas. I wrote out my plans in the "Book of Life" and was determined to stay clear of any incidents that might cast a shadow on my path to parole. Graduating from the culinary arts program would be a solid stamp on my record for the board to acknowledge.

When I wasn't in class or the library, you could find me working in the field, grinding on a tractor, or flipping cow shit into compost. Never in a million years would I have thought my source of joy would come from cow manure, yet being right in the middle of all its stink, the simple act of being outdoors independently was refreshing. It was a gentle reminder that if you have the willpower to transform, you can quickly turn what was once bullshit into something useful.

IMPLEMENTS OF ESCAPE

22

WHEN I WAS STILL IN SCI Graterford in 2010, I made a request to one of the guards I had a rapport with to keep my cell a transit cell—that is, to only put dudes in my cell that were staying for a week or two before they were transferred to another prison. I made this request because it would be the way to ensure two things: that I never got too comfortable with any of the men staying, and so that the movement would remind me that my time here was also temporary.

When you get to prison, you attempt to do anything you can to resist the routine. There's a long period of denial where, because you can't really believe this is your life, you disassociate with the process of being incarcerated and try to find ways to insist on whatever agency you have left. You try to find where you can make the experience feel as normal as possible. The ironic thing is that once you begin to normalize the experience, that's when you begin to accept the routine, and then you get comfortable.

Having different cellmates would prevent me from becoming too comfortable, but it would also provide me with some sidewalk therapy—stories from the outside. Anytime I'd get a new cellie, I'd immediately be like, "Damn, you cool man, you need anything?" And because the guy was still processing what happened to him, he ended up sharing with me stories about the free world that remind you of life outside. As your cellie grows more comfortable, they begin to share more about their lives outside prison, which then allows you more access to life beyond bars.

Once you've helped someone navigate those first few days where they need help with phone calls, getting cigarettes, and cosmetics, and they saw you ain't trying to take advantage of them, you become their therapist. They'll start talking about the side chicks they had in addition to their wives. They'd tell me about their trips to Miami and LA, telling me what cars they were driving, what restaurants they ate at, NBA games they went to, clubs they partied at, movies they watched, the color of the interior of their car, what they ordered at restaurants. And because I was so invested in these stories, I would turn into an interrogator, asking the most specific questions to get the most detailed answers.

One day, sometime in 2011, I was walking in the yard and saw this young boy from the neighborhood. Since I knew his mother, I reached out to her and let her know I saw her son and was going to look out for him. So I made sure he had some cosmetics, fresh underwear, whatever he needed, since he was just coming to prison. As I began building with him, doing my sidewalk therapy shit, he told me about this thing called Google.

Now, you must keep in mind that I was in prison since 2002, so the internet wasn't what it is now, and the world outside moved at a much more rapid pace. So he was telling me that Google was basically this search engine that can look up anything you can think of. The whole time I was listening to him, I was thinking he was on some bullshit. Sometimes the art of stretching the truth turns niggas into yoga masters in prison, the boredom of reality makes men inventive, and other times people on the outside just be running their mouths. This is what I thought the young bul was doing, especially when he told me this.

"I can even look you up."

This young nigga think because I've been in jail this long I'm slow.

"How the fuck," I ask the young bul, "can you look me up on some shit that I wasn't out in the free world for?"

This was a time before the internet was accessible in prison. Anything we wanted to learn came through television, the library, or buying books, so when the young bul shared what I thought to be make-believe, I had to take his word for it. It wasn't until maybe a couple of years later, in 2013, when my man Frank Nitty (RIP) came into my cell one day with a wireless hot spot and an iPhone Touch. I had only ever seen this shit on television at this point, so my mind was blown.

"What the fuck are you going to do with this?" I asked Frank.

Now, he's explaining to me that he uses it to listen to music, watch porn, and to google shit. At this point, I've been in for eleven years, so the first thing I'm thinking about was looking at porn. But I first wanted to see if the young bul was telling the truth, so I went to Google and typed in my name.

What the fuck?!

When I saw my name pop up, I dropped the phone. I thought the feds was watching me; I was scared to death. That night in my cell, after the initial fear of finding out that this Google shit gave me access to more than I wanted, I began thinking about what else

I could use it for. That's when I hit Frank about helping me get a phone.

In order to protect the innocent, I'm not going to share who on the outside got me the phone, but I'll share the means by which I received it. One day, I told the person visiting me to leave the wireless hot spot and iPhone Touch in the trashcan at the bottom of the hill. At this time I worked outside, cleaning up after all the other inmates went in. So I told this person to toss the hot spot and Touch in a McDonald's bag and throw it out like you would regular trash. I went down there, picked up the trash for the compound, and I was connected.

When I got the wireless hot spot and the phone, I began using the phone as an implement of escape. In prison, an implement of escape is a crime that charges you with having things that might aid your ability to physically escape prison on some *Shawshank Redemption* or *Life* shit. But I was using it to help me escape mentally. I used to be on there doing so much research, watching YouTube tutorials, Les Brown, and of course, porn. Life has a funny way of throwing you curveballs, and in the most unlikely of places, there in the trenches of a maximum-security prison, a friend of mine, Nitty, slipped me my golden ticket to the free world. Glancing at his cuffed hand, it was as if he was passing me a torch of freedom. It was an iPod Touch and with it, one of the most potent weapons to ever exist: a Wi-Fi hot spot. I'm not sure if Nitty realized that he had instantly become my unexpected savior in a sense, but I will be forever grateful for the tool he gave me that would change my life.

"You a bad muhfucka, Steve Jobs. Thank you, sir," I said as I held the tiny computer in the palm of my hand. For months, I found myself transported far beyond the barbed wire fences that stunted our knowledge of the outside world. This tiny device that could have easily made my life hell if patrol caught me with it brought endless amounts of game and intel that connected me with my future self in ways I could have never imagined. Being able to converse with anyone, anywhere, at any time through the internet was a bonus to the mounds of information I was learning by watching YouTube.

On the flip side, my enthusiasm for the benefits of having technology at the tip of my fingers got me into the telecommunications business. That's what we call hustling cell phones in the joint. Although risky, I used a third-party app to call around Philly to find a plug that would bring iPhones and iPods up for me to sell. Once that got rolling, I started to feel unstoppable.

Every chance I got, I would blow up Cousin Gillie's phone, running through idea after idea, things we would put together as soon as I touched the ground. Every call was a blueprint to weave through our dreams and schemes. These weren't your typical calls either; we didn't care about sharing what was going on in the streets or inside the belly of the beast. We sketched out major plays, from filming commercials to designing clothes. We talked about every detail down to the thread count we would use. That iPhone wasn't just a piece of tech; it was our headquarters.

Hiding cell phones on a nightly basis was a high-stakes game. Passing contraband off to other cellmates was a risk you sometimes had to take, but the rewards outweighed the fear of the consequences, so it was an easy decision to make. On nights I had the stash, it felt like I was sleeping next to ticking time bombs. It was a delicate dance with danger and a fine line between anxiety and anticipation, waiting to see who called or texted through the night when you weren't able to pick up the phone.

It was September 14, 2013, when I woke up to twenty-two missed calls. *Damn, something must be wrong,* I thought as I snuck a peek at the cracked pixelated screen on an iPhone 4. I was sure about one thing—nothing good happens after the clock hits a certain hour, and no good news comes afterward. I stared at the missed-call log, and my mind went straight to my grandmother. My greatest fear was that my Nanny wouldn't live to see me make it out of there. I shook my head in denial and shrugged off the unsettling thought. My body felt like it was drifting as I made my way to the dayroom, a place I had not ventured into much.

Channel 6 news was on the TV screen with the volume lowered almost to a hum. All I could see was the awning over a doorway on a block that looked just like Nanny's. "Turn it up, turn it up," I begged for the volume to be raised. I can remember these words blaring from the speaker like it was yesterday: "At one forty AM, a thirty-nine-year-old Black man was the fatal victim of gunshot wounds, one in the stomach, the other his head."

Right then and there, my ears felt as though they were filled with water, and a scream came roaring out of my soul, unlike anything I'd ever heard. Without hearing anything else, I knew it was my brother Steven who had been killed.

THE FIRST PERSON I CALLED to make sure it was true was my godsister. I didn't want to call Nanny or my mom immediately because I wanted to be sure that this was real before I called them with it. Between the two of us, Stevie and I had caused enough heartbreak, and I didn't want to create more. Once my godsister told me to call home, I knew this was real.

When I finally got to Nanny, she told me Steve went around the corner to the gas station to get a candy bar, and then Nanny heard shots. She headed to the door and saw Steve running down the street before collapsing inside the house. As soon as he stepped inside, he fell into her arms. Nanny told me she asked him, "What happened? Who shot you?" He looked up at her, and as he looked as though he was about to say something, his eyes rolled to the back of his head. Stevie died in Nanny's arms. Knowing how he died destroyed me. Not only was my brother violated, but my grandma had to see that.

After I got off the phone with Nanny, I called my mom, and all I remember were these visceral screams, her repeating, "They took my baby!" And I'm thinking, *These niggas killed Superman.* Because I was wilder, people thought I would die before him, and there I was, outliving my superhero.

State Police: Graterford inmate arrested for contraband

GRATERFORD – On May 21, 2014 state troopers conducting an investigation into contraband at Graterford Prison detained 34-year-old inmate Wallace Peeples and charged him with possession of contraband and weapons or implements of escape. Peeples was in possession of three cell phones, five chargers, five headsets, an iPod and a wireless hot spot. He was arraigned by District Judge Albert Augustine on June 10. Bail was set at $5,000.

IT HAD BEEN 4,215 DAYS since I was a free man, and I had another 1,143 days left before I'd be free again. I realized this as I sat in the hole of solitary confinement for a six-month stretch.

In an unannounced raid, state troopers stormed our cells in a hunt for illicit goods. I was later charged with possession of contraband and weapons or implements of escape. In other words, the troopers discovered the three cell phones, five chargers, five headsets, iPod, and wireless hot spot I had tucked away. Someone must have snitched and stuck it to me. I was sent to the hole.

In an unexpected twist of fate, the consequence of solitary confinement turned out to be something I drastically needed. My experience during those confined moments was oddly transformative. Unbeknownst to me, I had regressed in some ways and slid back into old patterns because of my unwillingness to accept my brother's passing. I became callous toward myself and others as my emotions were suspended in limbo. Denial made it impossible to confront the grief that had been haunting me since September 14, 2013, the day my hero got his wings.

It was a twisted blessing finding myself stuck in that cold box, forced to repent, forgive, grieve, and finally release the pain I had been dragging with me for so many years. In those lonely hours, I was able to face the suffering I was incapable of letting go of, as the system had stripped me of the chance to send my Steven off and bid him farewell. In the depths of isolation, I was able to mourn the loss of my big brother properly and finally navigate the maze of confusion that remained ever since my father disappeared and put both my heart and soul at ease.

And in the quiet of that storm, I was given another wake-up call: an inner voice urged me to evaluate the hurt all this had caused my mother—the hurt that I, too, caused my mother, my selfishness that led me to resent her for the weight of my father's absence and the impossible expectations I had of her to mend the agony I was hoarding. I freed her from the unrealistic burdens I placed on her shoulders. I wept through an epiphany that surfaced right when it was needed most. And in turn, I mentally freed myself as I whispered through my tears, "I love you, Mom. *I love you!*"

GOING BEFORE THE PAROLE BOARD was similar to stepping onto a battlefield. No matter how prepared and armored up you are, you never know which tactic the board members will use to disarm and attack you and your character. No preparation can shield you from their scrutiny, but I was fortified and equipped to lay my unfiltered truth on the table and accept whatever judgment came from it.

I was at peace with myself and the journey I'd been on to become the best man I could.

The faces of the board members were grim, and nothing I said seemed to move them in one direction or another. They were stern, cold, and, at times, dismissive when I would bring up the progress I'd made.

"Well, sir, I've completed my GED, I've earned a culinary certification, I've attended twelve-step programs, but bigger than that, I've facilitated workshops and study groups that helped several men get a better grasp on the realities of life, such as—" but before I could finish, I was cut off with another pointed question.

Parole Commissioner: Umm, it says here that you were found guilty of possession of contraband and weapons or implements of escape and were sentenced to disciplinary transfer and solitary confinement. What have you to say to that?

Inmate Peeples: I'd say I was guilty of possessing cell phones and their accessories, but they were not used negatively or for any thought of escape.

Parole Commissioner: What exactly were they used for then, Mr. Peeples?

Inmate Peeples: Well, Commissioner, my mission today was to be fully transparent and accountable, so if I am being sincere, I did a lot of research through YouTube on different businesses I could start if you offered me parole; I created a social media page @Wallo267 where I post positive messages about staying out of prison. You can look it up yourself and see. Oh, and porn. I did watch a good amount of porn, Commissioner.

□ □ □

THERE WAS A SILENCE THAT swept over the room and a shift in the board members' posture. I wasn't sure if I had overstepped and spilled too much raw truth, but I felt light as a feather and ready to face whichever direction their judgment would take me.

My closing statement felt no different from my talks with myself in the hole. There wasn't any applause for the long list of community service I planned to provide or the admission of remorse I'd come to know, whereas the man I once was had none to show. You could almost hear a pin drop, with the exception of the *tick-tock* from the clock on the wall.

After a short recess, the guard motioned for the mechanical door to open and brought me back inside the hearing room, but not before pressing me against the wall and frisking me for weapons, as if he hadn't frisked me several times already. Seriously, what was I going to do, find a secret stash of cell phones and toss it at somebody? For once, I just wanted to be treated as the man I'd become and not man-handled every step of the way as I pleaded for freedom.

The energy in the room was as tense as it was when we started the hearing. For a moment, I regretted how open I was and my promise to filter nothing. *Maybe I played a game of checkers while they were playing chess*, I thought. But in all honesty, I wasn't playing a game at all. I came in wanting to honor the journey I had been through, and I knew that meant showing up as authentically me.

Parole Commissioner: We've reconvened for the hearing of the panel's decision in the matter of Mr. Wallace Peeples. He is serving a 13.5 to 27-year sentence for armed robbery in the first degree. For the record, Mr. Peeples, this decision has not been easy for us. We were torn between the habitual past behaviors and the evidenced behavioral rehabilitation noted throughout your records. This decision was difficult with respect to the crimes committed and the lack of regard for human dignity. Although you may have absolved some issues personal to yourself during your sentence, it does not diminish the viciousness of the crimes you've committed against your community. With that said, the crucial question our panel must answer is whether you are still a potential threat to public safety. We have found the sufficient recording of reformative conduct and complete acceptance of your responsibility for your crimes to deem you suitable for parole.

TEARS FLOODED MY FACE WITHOUT warning. The commissioner continued with closing statements, but mentally, I had already escaped the confines of my shackles and left the room.

"Mr. Peeples," the commissioner called out.

"Yes, sir," I said, refocusing my attention on the panel.

"Off the record, your honesty, genuine expression, and desire to become innovative in serving the people brought balance to an otherwise gridlocked decision. Your potential is endless; please make something of the grace the board has given."

OVER THE NEXT NINETY DAYS, I dedicated myself to schooling anyone who would listen on what they needed to do to become suitable for release. I turned it up to the point where I could hear some of the guys jokingly say, "Aw shit, here comes Preacher Peeples," whenever I would walk in the room. But that didn't matter. I broke the code. I broke the curse. Reparations for my wrongs were paramount in my getting out and staying out.

In a bizarre twist of destiny, what had seemed like my biggest misstep, getting busted with cell phones, turned out to be a blessing in disguise. The unexpected transfer triggered the recalculation of my time, resulting in an entire year being shaved off my sentence. God bless the internet! Not only did it lead me to the den of my drastic evolution, but it was also the catalyst for my redemption!

ON SATURDAY, FEBRUARY 18, 2017, I crossed through the chained gates of hell into the land of the free.

The chill of the fresh air hit my lungs differently. I realized that even if we were out in the open yard, that was only an illusion of space, and the air we shared was still thick with painful stories of thirty-five hundred incarcerated men. I looked out the fogged window of the transport bus and thought, *Today is the day my life will begin!*

ARMED WITH GOOD INTENTIONS

ONCE THE EXCITEMENT OF MY welcome-home gatherings slowed down, I went right to work. One of the first videos I posted on social media was the one of $1,000 spread across a bed at Nanny's house in the middle room where I stayed. I opened the pages of the "Book of Life" and placed it in the middle so that it was visible from my iPhone lens. I pressed record, looked straight into the camera, and said, "Peep game, this is one thousand in cash. Now look, I just walked out of the penitentiary Saturday morning. I'm going to take this thousand that you see and this game in this book, all legit, and I'm going to turn this thousand into a hundred grand. I'm going to turn that hundred into a million, and I'm going to turn that million into a hundred million. You know what I'm going to do? I'm going to take care of my family and going to establish generational wealth. And if I can do it, you can. I've only been home for a few days, but I'm about to turn up. Don't ever let anyone tell you what you can't do, because if you can see it, you can be it."

That was February 24, just seven days after my release.

Some people thought I went crazy; many people just wanted to see the spectacle. Cousin Gillie had faith in me before I ever did, but he had to pump my brakes and get me straight on one thing before our mission started.

One of the songs I kept on repeat in my headphones was Bruce Springsteen's "Streets of Philadelphia." This song originally came out when I was around fourteen, and even then, when I was running the streets, I remember how much the song captured what living in Philly felt like.

In the jawn, Bruce sings about feeling beat down, being unable to recognize his own face when he looks in the mirror, and walking till he couldn't feel his legs anymore. When I came home, I was basically a loner. I would be downtown walking up and down Broad Street, walking around the city by myself. The only thing I had was me, my book bag, and my earphones with a couple dollars in my pocket to pay for the bus.

When I got out and I started doing my motivational videos around Philly and posting them on Instagram, I knew that I was battling with the content on other people's timelines. There was one thing I understood about getting people's attention: You got to make 'em laugh to make 'em listen. Social media is an attention game. Because the attention span is like eight seconds, I had to be able to make them forget about their thumbs, cause once someone remembered, their asses were scrolling again.

When I was in prison, there was this program called Real Street Talk. The purpose of the program was to give those of us who were already incarcerated the opportunity to give the newer inmates coming in some game, in hopes that some of them see the time they have as an opportunity to change the course of their lives. I was one of the speakers of Real Street Talk, where I might talk to a hundred or two hundred men. So many of my viral IG videos—with their intensity, passion, and clarity of vision—originated in Real Street Talk.

I can't remember what I spoke about exactly, but I do remember that one of the OGs, Brother Ali, was present. Ali used to do security for the Nation of Islam and was one of the men convicted of the Hanafi murders. The Hanafi murders took place in 1973, six years before I was born, when several members of the Black Mafia drove from Philadelphia to Washington, D.C., and shot two men and a young boy to death and drowned four children related to Hamaas Abdul Khaalis. Khaalis was a former member of the Nation of Islam who, after falling out with Elijah Muhammad, converted to Sunni Islam and tried to get other members of the Nation to leave. Khaalis is famous for getting Kareem Abdul-Jabbar, whose name was Lew Alcindor, to convert to Sunnism. The house where the massacre happened was at the home Abdul-Jabbar purchased for the Hanafi Muslims.

Brother Ali stayed in the cell next to mine. After one of my talks, Ali called me into his cell.

"What's up?" I asked him, standing in the door.

"Man, listening to you talk gave me chills. Reminds me of when Brother Malcolm was alive. I'm an older brother and I can understand that. But the young boys understand it, too. You speak with wisdom and with humor. Your delivery is so smooth and swift. When you go home, you better do something with that gift."

I can imagine some people rolling their eyes at the Malcolm X comparison, but to hear a man who knew Malcolm and heard him speak compare me to him was one of the batteries I needed. That's where the energy of those videos with me running in the rain in my socks, laying on the floor with ketchup on my forehead, pretending I was dead in a casket, telling people, "Don't wait until it's too late," came from. I was a man possessed—and some people had their opinions about it.

One day I'm at my cousin Gillie's house, and he gets a call from someone from the neighborhood we both know. When he calls Gillie, he doesn't know I'm there, so he starts talking shit about my videos.

"Yo, man, what's the matter with your cousin? Is he alright? That nigga crazy, man."

It wasn't the laughing that bothered me so much as the fact that I could tell by how he was laughing that the message went over his head. He only seemed to respond to how I was delivering what I was saying, not why, or even who I was talking to.

"Nah, cuz ain't crazy," Gillie responded. "He just doing his thing. He doing him."

After Gil hung up, he looked at me. "I ain't going to front, cuz. I ain't know what you was doing, but I knew you wasn't on no dumb shit, fucking around in the streets. You ain't come home mad, you ain't come on angry or none of that. So I had to support you. Keep doing your thing," he said.

A lot of times when dudes come home from prison, their energy be fucked up. They return home from a bid with this entitlement like they graduated from college with a PhD. They expect people to praise them for coming home and are often resentful when the same people who may have praised them at one point have moved on with their lives.

After I saw how quickly good intentions could lead me back to a cell, the last thing I was going to allow myself to feel was entitled. I remembered how my impatience when I lost that dice game in '02 led me to spend the next fifteen years of my life in prison. I wanted to do anything that was easy. I was thinking short. If you would've told me to bet a penny to win a million dollars that I'd be selling T-shirts at $20, $25, I'd have kept my penny and got some penny candy.

Gillie was right. I hadn't thought about it that way. I'd worked so hard to alter the image I once had that I felt I had to become a wordsmith to land my new message of transformation and positivity. But yeah, "Fuck that!" The streets that once knew my struggle will now witness raw determination and resilience from the ground up.

In the early stages, I didn't set out for financial gain. Although I needed money to survive first, then market and promote myself second, I took every dollar I made and dumped it back into the mission. I bought an old beat-down minivan, just something to get me from point A to point B, and started selling T-shirts and merch out of the trunk on the boulevard. With the money I earned, I created an LLC, bought a website domain, and trademarked my name, Wallo267. The "267" comes from my prison number. One of the effects of being institutionalized is associating my identity with how I was referred to. After years of hearing my name followed by the numbers, the name stuck.

Through my new journey, my relationship with my mother became a cornerstone in my development and the anchor that kept me grounded as my growth reached heights no one could have imagined. We often reflected on conversations we had during her visits to see me in prison, times when she would bring Steven's daughter and son, my niece Princess MayMay and my nephew Mukson, to visit. Each played a significant role in helping me remain dedicated to my goals. But my baby girl, Princess MayMay, sealed the deal.

"Uncle Wally, you have to be good when you get out of here, so you never come back and leave me," she once said. Those seeds planted and watered with their love and support were the nurturing elements that fortified me to return that love to the four corners of every hood.

After just twenty months of being home, I was offered a chance to speak on the massive media platform TED Talks. There was this sister named Nicole Purvy, a real estate investor, who had this space in North Philly where she'd work with kids, and it wasn't far from all the drug addiction and all that going on, heavy down in the Badlands. At first when I got out, I would try to shoot my shot at her, but she was focused on her work. Nicole was one of the people who not only took notice of what I was doing but also respected the approach I took to try to reach the people most vulnerable to the streets. One day I stopped by to see her and she told me about this brother from Atlanta named Jabari who organized TEDx talks. Nicole made him aware of my page, and he believed that what I had to offer was unique for their platform.

TED is this nonprofit that taps some of the most innovative and influential minds to share their knowledge with a broader audience. The videos are usually no longer than twenty minutes, but the topics are vast and their reach global. The TEDx talks were organized on a more local level, but the affiliation was official enough to signal that what I did on Instagram was working. At this time, I was doing speaking engagements for honorariums—$600 here, $1,000 there. If they're asking, I'm going. When Nicole explained to me what this opportunity was, I saw that this was bigger than money, but the chance to reach even more people on a platform where people who come from where I'm from don't typically reach. The opportunity was exciting and nerve-racking as I realized my demographic reach was quickly expanding. The key points the event organizer suggested were a conversation about life in prison and beyond, but deep down, my heart had different plans. Speaking to a broader audience would take courage to lift the veil and shine a light on a typically dark place where revenge is the default and embraced as the only possible option.

After talking with Jabari, and telling him I was down, he arranged a flight for me to go down to Buckhead, Atlanta, where they were having the event. In preparation, I watched a bunch of different videos to get a feel for the format and see what I could bring that no one else could or think to. I basically approached this like a rap battle. Friendly competition. I knew nobody was going to come like me on the aspect with the energy and the passion, and I wanted to make sure I picked a topic that people wouldn't only listen to but *feel*.

That evening, I took the stage with seven minutes to impact a room filled with individuals who may have never felt the disparities of living in underserved communities. TED Talks had over thirty-nine million subscribers on YouTube, so I knew I had one chance to convey the most vital testimony of my life. I took a deep breath and from my chest said, "I forgave my brother's killer."

AFTER WAKING UP IN SEPTEMBER 2013 to the news that Steven was killed, I felt victimized, violated, and terrified. To this day, I still don't know who killed my brother and for what reason. One thing I learned about situations like that is you never get the real story.

At the time, I also felt exposed because it was like all eyes were on me now. From the street mentality we grew up with in my neighborhood, especially with people knowing my brother, the unspoken expectation was that I had to do something.

In inner cities across America, retribution and revenge are strong motivators for the cycle of crime, death, and incarceration. When someone takes one of your loved ones, the pain is so deep that the only thing that seems logical is to make someone feel the loss you do. And knowing that those who resist retaliation are often seen as weak, I knew that the message of forgiving someone's killer would only resonate because it came from me, who was practicing what I was preaching. A lot of times the messages about how to navigate the hood come from people who aren't dealing with the same struggles, so hearing it from someone who ain't been through it is like someone who only played junior varsity trying to tell you how to make it to the NBA.

I had to forgive somebody that took a father from my niece and nephew; took a son from my mother; a grandson; my brother. I wanted to do this because I knew there were so many people who were overdosing on those potent drugs called resentment and revenge to avoid feeling the sobering pain of grief. I made a promise to myself to not seek vengeance on the man who took my brother. It helped that I would never know who it was, and I think it was incredibly helpful because not knowing forced me to deal with the vulnerability of pain without the distraction.

Before I forgave my brother's killer, I, like a lot of other people, believed that forgiving people felt like letting someone off the hook, like I was letting someone get away with something. If I hadn't forgiven the man who killed my brother, I'd probably still be looking for him, would've tried to kill him, and would either be dead or in prison. This entire process reminds me of hearing Jay-Z talk about how his pops left the family because he went looking for the man who killed his brother, Jay-Z's uncle. On the warpath, as Jay tells it, his father ends up getting hooked on heroin, and Jay isn't reunited with his father until decades later. I thought about it like this: Did I want to rob the people who cared about me of more time than they already lost with me in prison? When I did it, I realized forgiveness was a gift I gave to myself because it freed me to move on with my life. I gave myself permission to live.

□ □ □

EARLY ONE MORNING IN FEBRUARY 2019, I read this *Variety* article with the headline "Spotify Buys Podcast Startups Gimlet Media and Anchor, Plans Up to $500M in Acquisitions in 2019." The article revealed how Spotify would spend between $400 and $500 million on podcasts that year. Now I'm up and calling Gil.

"Yo nigga, read this article," I said when his voicemail picked up.

At first he didn't answer because he was asleep. After me calling him about ten times, he wakes up and tells me he's going to read it. Then he called me back.

"Yo, we got to do this. Let's get this shit."

By April, after getting the intellectual property, trademark lawyers, and legal shit handled, we launched our first episode of *Million Dollaz Worth of Game*. The first episode we did on my couch in my apartment in North Philly. Within the first seven hours we went to number two in comedy and number four overall on the podcast charts. Of course, these numbers inspired me to keep going, but I was shocked. Before that moment, I had never seen the impact of what I'd done happen so fast. Anytime you put out something new, you don't know how people are going to respond. And to avoid walking through old doors, I pushed it out of my mind that anything was going to come easy. Even though those numbers appeared seven hours after Gil and me releasing our first episode, I knew the reality that it really took thirty-nine years for me to see the kind of impact I could have. But what began as a lighthearted means of reaching out to communities worldwide and discussing life-changing experiences and sometimes brutal topics in comedic ways via our podcast became a breakout star in an oversaturated market of millions of shows.

The success of our show opened doors that were unforeseeable. Our energy and dynamic as loyal cousins, brothers, and friends changed the traditional tough-guy landscape in the hip-hop and urban corners of the world. The display of genuine love, affection, and the ability to talk major shit to each other without ever feeling a bit of disrespect is almost unheard of unless it is shown in parody. Together, we broke that mold—another generational curse broken.

Our childhood dreams of forming a rap super-group and touring the globe pivoted with the times. They propelled us into an influential space that allowed us to advocate for vulnerable populations from Philly to LA to the UK. We've become a globally recognized brand known for our philanthropic work and community service. I am not one to boast, but the podcast deal we struck with Barstool Sports was one of the most notable of its kind. Not only did we establish artistic authority over an unlikely collective (we are very Black, and they are very White), but we also met on mutual grounds of generosity and good intentions. And in a collaborative effort, post-pandemic, we committed $5 million to help affected small businesses.

"Armed with good intentions" is a phrase that is now part of my daily arsenal. When I realized that I was capable of more than I ever thought, that is when I learned to be resourceful and connect with people on a deeper level. Through self-reflection, I discovered that anything I put my mind to, I can eventually master. And through that discovery, I grasped the wisdom to make the most of what I had, which has always been *good intentions*. I've uncovered that if you genuinely want to be fully transformed, you must be one hundred percent intentional!

For the most part, the nut-ass decisions I've made in the past, the crimes that kept me hostage in severe consequential spaces for the better part of my life, were all driven by good intentions in one form or another. Yes, I wanted the material things that garnered attention (especially from the fine jawns around Philly), but I also wanted to be the man of my house and help provide for my family and others. I always wanted to be a part of something bigger and better than what I learned on the cruel streets of Philly, but those were all the reasons I needed to involve myself in stupid shit and try to be someone other than who I was meant to be.

There were days when I wanted to give up, let my mind slip, quit, or worse. There were moments when the days got so tough that I wanted to curl up in my bunk and take one of those forever naps. You know, the ones there's no coming back from. But those thoughts never lasted more than a minute or so because the voice in my head, maybe God, or whatever it was, never allowed me to fold and always reminded me to keep going.

"No one will save you," I quietly screamed to myself daily. This statement was a constant reminder that my purpose was not only bigger than me and my love for my family, but it was my love for the world's humans as far as I could reach. And *those* were the people that needed me to heal myself.

I am a changed man with a new perspective and an unquenchable thirst to continue learning and developing myself and others to be better than their circumstances. I've been battle-tested and proven resilient! I show no mercy when it comes to fulfilling my purpose. My life has been dedicated to using my experiences to inspire others to never give up, no matter how hard or how fucked up the road may seem. Over the years, I've encountered more people on the outside tragically paralyzed by fear of past situations. I'd swear their negative thoughts held them back far more than any prison could. But this is what this book is about, pushing through and having the determination to conquer the days ahead while being one hundred percent authentically you.

So if you're feeling stuck or facing insurmountable challenges, I want you to know that you can make it through anything, just like I did, as long as you never give up on fighting for yourself.

This book is my story, my journey from a scared, dysfunctional kid, a seemingly lost soul, to a beacon of hope and a man of integrity, from terrorizing the streets of Philly to being honored by the Philadelphia mayor as a changemaker and positive impact on the very city that raised me. None of this has been easy or pretty. But it was real, and it was vulnerable.

PRESS RELEASE: February 13, 2024

REFORM Alliance Appoints Wallace "Wallo267" Peeples to Serve as Organization's New Chief Marketing Officer

NEW YORK, FEB. 13, 2024 /PRNEWSWIRE/ – Today, REFORM Alliance formally announces the appointment of Wallace "Wallo267" Peeples to lead the organization's marketing department as Chief Marketing Officer. Peeples will be responsible for the development of REFORM's long-term marketing strategy, activations, and brand in-novation. Peeples will play a critical role as the organization continues to further its commitment to transform supervision by changing laws, systems, and culture to create real pathways to work and well-being.

IN LATE 2023, MEEK MILL FaceTimes me.

"Yo, what's up? Mike Rubin called me and told me they're thinking of bringing you into REFORM on marketing."

REFORM Alliance is the nonprofit organization founded by Jay-Z, Michael Rubin, CEO and founder of Fanatics, the global digital sports platform, American investor Michael Novogratz, social justice advocate Clara Wu Tsai, and hedge fund manager Daniel S. Loeb. REFORM is particularly focused on changing laws that affect probation, parole, and sentencing—all things I've experienced firsthand. So when Meek told me that I had a chance to run the marketing for an organization that was working overtime for people like me, I didn't hesitate.

Mike Rubin shared with Meek that he saw me as a one-man self-marketing agency. He liked the way I promoted my clothes and delivered my message. I get on there and I do it myself.

"Mike said he asked Jay what he thinks," Meek continued. "Jay agreed."

To hear how much faith everyone placed in me felt affirming. I told Meek hell yeah, and two days later, Mike hit me up directly. He put me on text with his executive assistant. After that, I got with my business manager, Des. Something I respected and was touched by was the respect they regarded her with. As I've moved up and through the professional world, I've seen the subtle ways people undermine those of us who they feel aren't as established as they are. They do little shit like forget to include people on emails or insist on messaging me even after I've directed them to Des. So it was important to me that they gave Des what I feel she rightfully earned.

The first time we met was at Fanatics to talk about what joining REFORM would look like.

"Listen Wallo," Mike told me. "You're a great marketer. And you connect, you connect with people we want to reach. You are raw, you're organic, it's real. It's not forced. We need you here at REFORM to be the chief marketing officer. What does that look like to you?"

I thought I was just going to go there and do some campaigning—I wasn't expecting to run the whole division. But this is what I studied in prison. For me to be certified with this title itself is the co-sign that I know what I'm doing. That meeting was an emotional moment for me because I went from putting ketchup on my head telling people, "Don't wait until it's too late" as a viral stunt to getting a corporate-level job offer. I have no college degree or MBA, and yet here I am.

This appointment validated not just me but the people the world has forgotten about. I always feel like I represent them—the people who might live in poor and neglected neighborhoods, the people who went to jail, the people who fell in life, the people who are addicted to drugs and trying to recover. And I felt so powerful, like I'm showing them, *Look what we've done.* The possibilities after prison are the possibilities after failure. It's the possibility to win after the loss.

"Because I know you got a lot of stuff going on," Mike continued, "I don't want all your time. I just need half your time to be able to be on top of this and really bring this to life."

A couple of months later, Des and I went to Mike's crib outside Philly on a Saturday morning and the house was amazing. There was a lake, a bridge, a basketball court next to a tennis court, and a swimming pool, all inside the gate. We met up with the CEO, Robert Brooks, who broke down everything, and on the first day of February, I stepped into my position.

When I think about the fact that I was appointed to REFORM

just a couple of weeks before the seventh anniversary of my release, I know anything is possible. Though I'm forty-five, with twenty-four years left till I'm off parole, I am grateful for the fact that I've already beat so many odds. And with every year, I'm further from going back. With every year, I'm one step closer to taking back my freedom.

I just want to take this time to thank everyone who ever helped me during my journey through life. You are all greatly appreciated in ways unimaginable!

With love,

Wallo267